Appalachian Anthology:

Histories, Historiographies, and Oral Histories of Appalachia

Appalachian Anthology: Histories, Historiographies, and Oral Histories of Appalachia and Southern Settlers

Edited by Diane Alexander

1. Appalachian Region, Southern
2. Appalachian Settlers
3. Appalachian Dialect
4. Appalachian Speakers
5. Appalachian Life
6. Oral Histories
7. Dialect Stigmata
8. Stereotypes
9. Media
10. Identity Construction
11. Appalachian Music
12. Appalachian Identity
13. Moonshine
14. World War II
15. Scottish Highland Games
16. Scottish Highlands
17. Highland Clearances
18. Ethnography
19. Diaspora
20. Native American Removals
21. Ethnic Cleansing
22. Emigrants
23. Coca-Cola
24. Civil War
25. Scottish Highland genealogy and ethnic history

A collection of Appalachian journal articles, research papers, historiographies, and oral histories prominently featuring Appalachian culture, dialect, and stereotyping. Vignettes of oral history from the 30s and 40s will charm and amuse the reader, highlighting the observation that Appalachians are both natural-born storytellers and humorous.

Appalachia has fought harder than most other American cultures in establishing an evenhanded reputation, dispelling various stereotypes such as being the land of hillbilly backwardness with a culture of harsh poverty and illiteracy that has entrapped its people, and enriching and preserving its heritage. Scholars who supported the poverty-stricken image of the Appalachians claimed their research revealed an oppressive culture that imprisoned its people.

In contrast, histories, historiographies, and oral histories from Appalachia demonstrate that the people made their culture; the culture did not make the people.

Appalachian Region and Oral Histories

The Forties

Joseph Alexander

I was born on October 14, 1938 in Fairview, North Carolina. I don't remember this event, but believe it to be factual and accurate. Life was very settled and routine for a couple of years and then upheaval threatened my serenity. We moved to Newport News, Virginia. From the conversations around me, I believed that we were going far, far away to a land populated by very odd people. We referred to our future home as "Newpertnews." The Alexander family was about to embark on a disjointed journey through the unsettled Forties, a very different decade.

Before the move, Pappy had been working as a deputy sheriff. He didn't like his job, so he enrolled in welding school at Canton with a plan to apply for work at the shipyards in the Norfolk, Virginia area. The shipyards were hiring and expanding due to the deteriorating world situation and, compared with the work opportunities in our area, presented a lure that could not be denied. Pappy graduated, was promised a shipyard job, and then we were off to foreign soil in our 1940 Chevrolet and a friend-owned truck full of our belongings. I made the trip in a bed on the rear shelf above the back seat of the car as that was the only space in the car that was not packed with our household goods. Pappy had gone to Newport News before the move to apply for a welding job at the shipyard, but had been hired as a "burner" instead. A burner made cuts in huge sheets of steel with an acetylene cutting torch, and these cut sheets would then become part of a new or a battle-damaged ship. After being hired, Pappy found us a place to live - a new, two-story, two-bedroom house, and we moved our stuff and us into it. There were five of us so the bedroom assignments might have been a thorny issue. I know I always had a bed, so I suppose I didn't pay too much attention to the other folk's sleeping arrangements. To make the bedroom assignments more difficult, WE TOOK IN BOARDERS. Other men from the Asheville area had also gone to welding school and then to Newport News. Some did not move their families there, at least right away, and we took a couple of them in as boarders. I don't believe we ever had more than one boarder at a time which might have helped the bedroom situation some, but still it had to be a tight schedule. Also, the shipyard worked on a shift basis so we had people sleeping while others were out of their respective beds. (The Navy refers to this procedure as "hot bedding"). One of the boarders was George Davis who became Pappy's lifelong friend and entertained the family with his wit and antics over the years. George had been given a welding job at the shipyard, but this apparent competitive advantage over Pappy didn't seem to dampen the friendship between them.

One household item that did not make the Fairview to Virginia cut was my baby bed which had been unceremoniously dumped in the swamp next to our house. It was a nice, secure iron bed, and I missed it. Buh felt sorry for me and said she would have never thrown my bed away if she had known how attached I was to it. I filled the psychological loss of the bed with thumb-sucking which seemed to disturb the rest of the family a great deal. The efforts to make me quit this habit went on for several years, and all members of the family took a shot at solving my compulsion. I didn't see it as a compulsion, but simply as a baby bed replacement therapy. Bruce was sure he had the answer when he dipped my thumb in red pepper. With tears running down my cheeks, I licked away the pepper and resumed my primary therapeutic activity. My mouth burned for days after that, but I had my thumb to compensate and comfort me through my period of distress. Buh fussed at Bruce and would not let him try that "fix" or any other thumb-sucking cessation plan after that.

Then a metal cage that fit over my thumb and tied around my wrist was brought into the battle. I defeated this strategy by removing the strings and hiding the cage as soon as I was out of sight of my antagonists, and I was back in business. During this protracted period of failed attempts to alter my unpleasant habit, it surprises me that no one ever tried the one stratagem that would surely have succeeded - the return of my bed! As time went on and efforts to stop my thumb-sucking continued, I became less interested in my thumb and more involved in activities that required two hands (such as eating, tricycling, home destruction, etc.) so I quit. All members of the family seemed to take credit for my lifestyle correction, and I saw no harm in letting them think that. I've been told by dentists that something in my early life had left me with a dental over-bite. I believe it was the red pepper.

We became acclimated, if not completely comfortable with our new life in Newport News. Roy and Bruce were enrolled in school. I made friends with the kid next door, Mike Spangler. The war became worse and I was scared at times. We had blackouts during recurring air raid drills, and when we inadvertently left a bathroom light on one night during a drill, we received a fine by the local wartime authority. (After the war, it was admitted that there was virtually no threat of an air attack on the east coast shipyards because the distance to the nearest enemy occupied airfield exceeded the maximum range of any airplane of that era.) We sold the '40 Chevrolet. Gas was rationed and I guess it was decided there was no reason to keep the car, and this began a long period when we had no automobile at all. Mike Spangler and I became more and more worried about the war situation. I think there was a feeling among the general populace that we might be losing the war as there were constant government pleas for all of us to do more to help the war effort, i.e., plant victory gardens, conserve critical goods, recycle cans and paper. Mike and I took these public involvement programs very seriously and decided that we should go to Germany to help our boys fight. We collected our weapons, some fearful sticks and menacing stones, put them in a wash tub with a pull-string attached and told Buh that we were going to Germany to fight the war. Buh gave us her blessing as she always did for whatever endeavor we chose then or any other time in our lives, and we departed for the front. We knew that Germany was across the ocean and the nearest water (not the ocean, but we didn't know or care about the difference) was about ten blocks away, so we set a course for the Chesapeake Bay dragging the tub with our weapons of mass destruction. We got to the Bay to find that someone or some power had constructed a chain-link fence to keep forces such as ours out. About the time we were formulating plans to breach the barrier, Mr. and Mrs. Spangler drove up. (The Spanglers had not sold their car.) We were loaded up and returned home for a severe lecture on crossing streets. The standing rule had been that we could go anywhere in the neighborhood as long as we didn't cross a street, but my defense was based on the disclosure I had made that we were bound for Germany. It should have been obvious that streets would have to be crossed, and I still believe that to be a good defense.

Pappy became more homesick as time passed. When he couldn't stand being away from home anymore, he planned a trip back to visit Granddad, Granny, his sisters and his mountains. For reasons that I have never known, he decided (or was told) to take me with him on the trip. It might have been that Buh needed a rest from me. I rode a train for the first time, and fell in love with the huge, black, smoke and cinder belching, steam-powered locomotives. To add to the experience, we had Pullman accommodations and our meals were served in the dining car. The trip was marred only by a minor incident in Richmond where we were scheduled for a train change. We had to walk across several tracks to get to our train and that's where we learned that my foot (shoe) was exactly the same size as the gap between the rails and the platform. I became stuck in the tracks of a very busy rail yard. Recognizing that time was of the essence, Pappy grabbed my leg and pulled with some urgency. That freed my foot but left the shoe still firmly stuck in the rails - and shoes were rationed and expensive. The shoe fit so nicely in the rails that its extraction was not easy, but before the next train was scheduled for that particular track, my traveling companion had retrieved the shoe, relieved my semi-shoeless condition, and hustled me off to our train bound for the mountains.

I was asleep in my Pullman berth when Pappy awakened me the next morning. We were in the mountains and he was excited. He told me that we would soon be going through the tunnels of Black Mountain (just east of Asheville) and he didn't want me to miss it. We went to the dining car and I had French toast for the first time. I thought it was the most wonderful food I had ever tasted. Then the tunnels came up and that was exciting as the train went from daylight to dark in an instant as it barreled through the coal smoked cavern. It seemed like there was no sense of movement until, as suddenly as the dark had come, daylight would return and I would look forward to the next tunnel. Soon after the tunnels we pulled into the Biltmore train station and then on to Fairview with our relatives. I think this homesick trip may have triggered a permanent return to the mountains for the Alexander family.

Meanwhile, life went on in Newpertnews as the war continued its mayhem around the world. With Pappy's shipyard pay we were able to buy essentials, a few items we considered luxuries, and as Buh was to say later, we were able to save some money for the first time. Our savings were in the form of War Bonds. Everyone had War Stamp books that, when filled with war stamps, could be exchanged for bonds. The stamps were in all the denominations of U.S. currency so, on occasion, I would be given a penny or a nickel or a dime stamp and would get a charge out of licking them and sticking them in my stamp book. To add to the interest, the pages of the stamp book had scenes of Japanese or German forces attacking our troops or ships, and by covering these evil scenes we were taking an active role in the war. By1944, living in a foreign land had become too much for Pappy and we quit the shipyard, loaded up our stuff, and returned to the mountains. This decision must have been a hurried one, because we had no house to live in when we returned to Fairview. We had rented our Fairview house to the Padgett family from West Asheville, and they were still living in it with no plans of leaving. Marguerite (Alexander) Fortune and her husband, Charles, had built a small log house on a piece of Granddad's property which they used as an occasional home away from their Asheville home, and we moved into their log home awaiting the Padgett's move out of ours. Marguerite's log home was not luxurious, but very comfortable and I really liked it. The house was built in a particularly pretty part of the woods and it was blessed with a very cold and prolific spring that came to the surface through the moss and ferns in front of the house. It was living here that I began an enduring and ardent love for the forest. I spent most of my outside time in the woods, finding and opening new springs, watching animals, and listening to the sounds and absorbing the smells of the trees and plants. One of my regular stops in the woods was to stand in awe and fear over the supposedly hidden grave of a Union soldier who, whispers had it, was killed while scavenging during the war. I always regretted the time when I had to leave the woods for a return to civilization, and there were times when I had to be called in by a family member with a voice strong enough to be heard over some distance.

I was five years old and fall was approaching which meant that classes would be starting soon at Fairview School. I was not to start school that year because of my age, however

Buh was offered a teaching job at Fairview School and she accepted it on the condition that I be allowed to begin school early. The deal was approved and we both started school together. She did better on the first day than I - she didn't cry (I don't think). We still had no automobile so we rode to school with Aliene (Alexander) Ashworth in her 1942 Ford. Pappy had taken a job again as a deputy in Asheville, but he had no means of getting to work, so he bought a very used, very well worn-out 1933 Ford sedan. So the 1940 Chevrolet had now been replaced with a 1933 Ford, and later when the '33 Ford died completely, it was replaced with a 1929 A Model Ford. This was the end of the line for our retrogressive auto acquisitions because there simply weren't any used cars older than our Model A.

We lived in Marguerite's home for about a year and then moved back to our Fairview home after the Padgetts finally vacated the premises. The house was in bad condition after the rental so we had to replace, paint and repair before we could move in, but we were back in our home by the time the war came to an end in 1945. Bruce and I held a victory celebration in our front yard after the radio announcement that the war was finally over. We needed fireworks, but all we had were pans and tubs to beat on, and so we did.

The decade was drawing to a close. Pappy didn't like working as a deputy sheriff any better this time around than he had before our move to Newport News, so he decided to start a dairy business. His impatience with animals (and some folks) made his sisters wonder if that was a good decision, but his mind was set and the dairy plan was set into motion. He gave up his deputy badge, cashed in his war bonds, borrowed construction money from Asheville Production Credit Association and Biltmore Dairy Farms, and jumped into the entrepreneurial arena. We built the dairy barn with most of our own materials and all of our own labor. The cement blocks were made on a block-making machine we had bought from Montgomery Ward. The foundations and cement floors were poured using a second-hand cement mixer we had picked up at a bargain price. All the lumber used in the barn was oak that we had cut, hauled and sawed into lumber at Granddad's mill. Pappy drew the plan for the barn on some brown paper bags, and the plan seemed to change from day to day once construction started. Eventually the building was pronounced ready for the commencement of dairy operations, and we bought six reluctant Holstein cows that had been shipped into the area from Wisconsin. Someone in the family wondered why those cows were sold in Wisconsin if they were without problems, and it soon became obvious that the cows did have some quirks, but they also produced a lot of milk - if you could get in from them. They kicked, bit, bawled, pooped, and glared as twenty to thirty pounds of milk was painfully taken from each of them twice a day. I figured Wisconsin didn't sell them because they were poor producers, but because the product was not worth the process. To make the situation more ironic, Bruce had given the cows flower names - Hydrangea, Geranium, Delphinium, etc. The names just didn't fit their personalities. The herd would eventually grow to about twenty cows, but none were purchased from Wisconsin after the "Cantankerous Six" experience and none were given flower names.

After the extended startup period for our business, we finally received our first monthly milk check from Biltmore Farms. It was for $12.65. I was elated, but others in the family business were not so ecstatic. My reasoning told me that $12.65 was infinitely better than our income over the entire time we were building the barn. The more practical members of the family wondered how we would pay off our loans with such small revenues. The checks grew some after we paid Biltmore Farms the money they had loaned us to get started. "We owed our soul to the company store."

And then it was 1950, and the Alexander's journey through the Forties had come to an end. During that decade there were many events and circumstances that affected our lives and those of other families. Many families moved away from their birthplace to find work and then remained where they had moved, but that could have never been our fate. In our family there existed an influence that had more to do with our life than the war or the economy. That influence never weakened nor waned throughout that decade or those that followed. It was a force that could not be denied and one that had to be accepted and accommodated. It severely limited the time we could be away from the mountains. Pappy's mountains demanded our presence.

Appalachian Youth in World War II: An Oral History

Diane Alexander

Far from the European battlefront, World War II had a profound effect on the American home front. It also had a monumental effect on Appalachian youth. Wartime experiences inevitably vary hugely depending on a child's age and specific events and dynamics germane to the child's family. For Appalachian youths, who came of age during World War II, their experiences and remembrances greatly differed as well. Some remembered a united time, full of adventure and new things; while others saw their families dislocated, or broken by fathers, brothers, and uncles who never returned from the war. Still other youths found their familial bonds strengthened and experienced the infancy of their love for Appalachian homelands during these fluctuating times.

Anna Wolf and Irma Simonton Black in "What Happened to the Younger People," claim younger children, particularly those up to six years old, knew less about the war but were the most deeply affected.[1] These were crucial

---

[1] Anna Wolf and Irma Simonton Black, *What Happened to the Younger People,* quoted in Marilyn M. Harper, *World War II & the American Home Front: A National Historic Landmarks Theme*

formative years for these youths, and their lives would be forever structured by their wartime experiences in 1940s United States. According to Wolf and Black, five and six year olds "felt directly the tumult as well as the excitement of home front life."[2] Glen H. Elder, Jr., a pioneering sociologist of lifespan and human development studies, concurs with the impact of wartime on the youths, stating that human lives are shaped "not only 'by the settings in which they are lived,' but also 'by the timing of encounters with historical forces, whether depression or prosperity, peace or war.'"[3]

One such Appalachian youth, Joseph Richard Alexander, who was four at the time of the United States' entry into the war, recalls his childhood memories of World War II, remembering that many events and circumstances immeasurably affected their lives and those of other families during that decade. He prefaces his remembrances with, "The Alexander family was about to embark on a disjointed journey through the unsettled Forties, a very different decade."[4] Joe's father, William Cruser Alexander, known by both family and

---

Study, (Washington, D.C.: Department of the Interior, 2007), 70.

[2] Wolf, *What Happened to the Younger People*, 70.

[3] Glen H. Elder, Jr., *Social History and Life Experience* quoted in Marilyn M. Harper, *World War II & the American Home Front: A National Historic Landmarks Theme Study*, (Washington, D.C.: Department of the Interior, 2007), 71.

[4] Joseph Richard Alexander, *The Forties* oral history interview by author, August 2008.

acquaintances as Pappy, was working as a deputy sheriff in Asheville, North Carolina in the early 1940s. Pappy was a fifth generation North Carolinian, whose farmlands had been in the family of Alexander settlers since the early 1700s. For the Alexander family, the pull of the land was more powerful than any depression or war ever faced in their homeland. The rise of defense jobs, however, enticed Pappy to enroll in a welding school in order to apply for work in the shipyards in Newport News, Virginia. He was offered a position as a burner at the Newport News Shipyard. A burner cut huge sheets with an acetylene torch, which were used for new construction of ships or to repair ships.

World War II was a watershed for Appalachian outmigration, as the economy lured tens of thousands of Americans from their homelands to defense jobs in urban areas, as far away from Appalachia as Chicago and Detroit. In addition, tens of thousands Appalachians enlisted in the armed forces. The promise of greater economic security and better living conditions attracted thousands of Appalachians, who for many had only known poverty and hard times, toward an opportunity for a better life. For some, these new urban areas would become their new home; for others, they would be drawn back, regardless of the distance or time spent away from their homelands. Pappy was one such Appalachian who could not deny his connection to his homeland and would remain a resident of the region his entire life. Despite the willingness to move away for an opportunity to work in a defense job, he did not sell his farm, but rather rented it out, indicating his full intention to adjust with the wartime economy for only as long as necessary. The outmigration of those who permanently moved away had lasting effects on the region. In "Uneven Ground: Appalachia since 1945," by Ronald Eller, a mountain teacher remarked, "The young manhood of our town has moved out almost en masse…Never again can this section be the same."[5] Today, Appalachia remains a blend of its past legacy, including remaining pockets of poverty endemic in certain Appalachian areas and modern industrialization and development in others, along with the permanent demographic shift from the mass migration prominent during World War II.

Pappy and his wife Ruth, known by all as Buh, with their three sons, Roy, Bruce, and Joe, moved from their Fairview (a western town on the outskirts of Asheville), North Carolina home to Washington Avenue in Newport News, Virginia in 1942. Their eldest son, Roy, was fourteen, Bruce was ten, and the youngest, Joe, was four. Newport News, Virginia was a boomtown during World War II, as it also had been during World War I. Its main thoroughfare was Washington Avenue. Pappy went to work for his new employer, the Newport News Shipyard, where a huge banner spanned the factory floor, with several patriotic slogans

---

[5] Ronald D. Eller, *Uneven Ground: Appalachia since 1945,* (Lexington: University Press of Kentucky, 2009), 8.

imprinted, one in particular, "Help to Sink the Rising Sun," reminding the workers of their important work contributions. The shipyard constructed and delivered 47 fighter ships to the U.S. Navy during World War II, 185 service ships, and repaired hundreds of damaged ships, as well, during wartime.[6]

Their remembrances of the war were diverse. The oldest son, Roy, recalls looking for a job soon after arriving. Jobs for youth were scarce and he applied to a grocery job at Pender's Meat Market. Fearing a job denial, when the manager asked Roy his age, he replied sixteen, even though he was only fourteen. Marilyn Harper in "World War II and the American Home Front" confirms this common occurrence, stating, "Thousands of young people went to work. In 1940, for example 900,000 Americans between the ages of fourteen and eighteen were employed. By the spring of 1944, their number had climbed to 3 million – one-third of their age group."[7]

Roy recalls the numerous war posters in the store, including one that warned, "Loose lips sink ships," and another, "Lucky Strike Green has gone to war." Roy worked there after school and on Saturdays. The market collected ration points for meat and collected fats for wartime salvage.

---

[6] William A. Fox, *Downtown Newport News*, (Mount Pleasant: Arcadia Publishing, 2010), 16.

[7] Marilyn M. Harper, *World War II & the American Home Front: A National Historic Landmarks Theme Study*, (Washington, D.C.: Department of the Interior, 2007), 72.

Families were encouraged to save cooking grease in cans and bring them back to stores. The glycerin in fats was used to make explosives. In addition, turning in fats earned extra ration points.[8] Roy explains that they did not collect fats on their busiest day, and remembers with humor his putting a sign in the window saying, "Ladies, please do not bring your fat cans here Saturdays!" He recalls graffiti in the stockroom left over from the Depression era, "Hoover is my shepherd – and I want."[9]

For Roy, the move to Newport News in his teen years instilled in him a sense of adventure and the excitement of new places. Although he did not realize it at the time, this move would begin the first footsteps along his career path. Once the war was over, Roy continued living the urban life, going next to Holyoke, Massachusetts and then "inexorably drawn" to New York City, where he remained a resident for the remainder of his life.[10] The others of the William Alexander family would return to their Appalachian roots, and even though both Bruce and Joe would move away for their careers, both commercial airline pilots, both sons would return to their Appalachian roots upon retirement. They each settled in

---

[8] Richard Panchyk, *World War II for Kids: A History*, (Chicago: Chicago Review Press, 2002), 50.

[9] Roy Alexander, *Power Speech: The Quickest Route to Business and Personal* Success, (New York: AMACOM, Division of American Management Association, 1986), 5.

[10] Alexander, *Power Speech*, 5.

Tennessee on the western side of their Smokey Mountains childhood home, where Bruce lived until his death in 2001, and where Joe still resides.

Joe remembers their arrival in Newport News, Virginia in 1942, relating, "After being hired, Pappy found us a place to live – a new, two-story, two-bedroom house, and we moved our stuff and us into it. There were five of us so the bedroom assignments might have been a thorny issue. I know I always had a bed, so I suppose I didn't pay too much attention to the other folk's sleeping arrangements. To make the bedroom assignments more difficult, *we took in boarders!*"[11] There was a shortage of housing in the Hampton Roads area and demand could not keep up with the supply. Other men from the Asheville area had also gone to welding school and then on to Newport News. Some of them did not move their families there, at least right away, and the Alexanders took a couple of them in as boarders. Joe does not recall ever having more than one boarder at a time, but states it still had to be a tight schedule. He recalls the process Navy refers to as "hot bedding" whereby many shipyard employees, who worked shifts, would sleep while others were at work, thus rotating the sleeping accommodations.

During World War II, communities in coastal areas would conduct air raid drills. Given the recent events of the

---

[11] Alexander, *The Forties* oral history.

London Blitz – bombing by the Germans – and the Japanese attack on Pearl Harbor, the threat of being bombed was a legitimate, real fear. In areas with air raid drills, a siren would sound, signaling a drill. Everyone would have to pull their window shades down, turn off all lights, and remain inside. If people were driving, they had to pull over and shut off their car and lights. Authorities throughout the areas would ensure everyone was following instructions. In the Hampton Roads area, air raid drills were common. In 1942, German U-boats in the Atlantic Ocean fired torpedoes at whatever they could, including non-military targets. Oil, fuel, and wreckage often came ashore in the Hampton Roads area.[12] Joe recalls these drills. "The war became worse and I was scared at times. We had blackouts during recurring air raid drills, and when we inadvertently left a bathroom light on one night during a drill, we received a fine by the local wartime authority."[13]

Appalachians were well known for their patriotism and always ready to serve their country in wartime. Enlistment rates in Appalachia were among the highest in the nation during World War II. Joe remembers the frequent government pleas for all citizens to do more to help the war effort, such as plant victory gardens, conserve, and recycle cans and paper. Victory gardens were encouraged patriotic tasks; their purpose

---

[12] Patrick Evans-Hylton, *Hampton Roads: The World War II Years*, (Mount Pleasant: Arcadia Publishing, 2005), 51.
13 Alexander, The Forties oral history

for families to grow their own food and help prevent shortages and conserve rationed goods. They were also a good way for everyone, particularly the children, to participate in the war effort.[14] Another community war effort for children was collecting scrap metal, newspaper, and aluminum foil. Richard Panchyk, in "World War II for Kids," writes of a youth, Joan, who recalls collecting aluminum foil as the most fun activity. She explains kids would collect foil, often from gum wrappers and cigarette packs, and make them into balls of foil. Kids would compete to see who could make the biggest ball of foil on the block.[15]

Joe became friends with Mike Spangler, a boy his age who lived next door to them on Washington Avenue. He recalls that Mike and he decided that they should go to Germany to help "our boys fight." Explaining their preparation, "We collected our weapons, some fearful sticks and menacing stones, put them in a washtub with a pull-string attached and told Buh that we were going to fight the war. Buh gave us her blessing as she always did for whatever endeavor we chose then or any other time in our lives, and we departed for the front. We knew that Germany was across the ocean and the nearest water - not the ocean, but we didn't know or care about the difference - was about ten blocks away, so we set a course of the Chesapeake Bay dragging the tub with our

---

[14] Panchyk, World War II for Kids, 49.
[15] Panchyk, *World War II for Kids*, 52.

weapons of mass destruction."[16] After reaching the bay, they discovered a chain link fence on the beach shore prevented them from going any further. While trying to figure out how to breach this barrier, Mike's parents drove up and returned the boys home. Joe recalls receiving a severe lecture about crossing streets. The rule was that the boys could go anywhere in the neighborhood as long as they did not cross any streets. Joe feigns outrage remembering the scolding, justifying that after all they had disclosed to Buh that they were bound for Germany. It should have been clear that in order to fulfill that mission, streets would have to be crossed. He chuckles, stating he still believes that to be a good defense.

During World War II, the government enacted rationing methods, the most common of these ration books, which would go through four editions during World War II. When Ration Book 1 first circulated, sugar was the only food rationed, and you could not get change for a stamp. By the time Ration Book 4 was issued in 1943, coffee, meat, butter, and various canned goods were included in rationed goods; and you could get change from ration stamps in the form of tokens. Each person received an allotment of 48 blue points and 64 red points per month, not including the tokens that could be saved up by receiving change. Red tokens were to be used for meat, fish, and dairy products, and blue tokens for canned goods. The

____

back of Ration Book 4 admonished citizens to "Never buy rationed goods without rationed stamps," in addition to warning, "Never pay more than the legal price."[17]

Joe recalls that with Pappy's shipyard pay, they were able to buy essentials and even a few items they considered luxuries. Able to save money for the first time in their lives, they had war stamp books that, when filled with stamps, could be exchanged for War Bonds. He recalls the stamp collecting process, a patriotic process in which even the youngest family members could participate. The stamps were in all the same denominations as U.S. currency, so occasionally he would be given a penny, nickel, or dime stamp and he would get a charge out of licking them and sticking them in his stamp book. "To add to the interest, the pages of the stamp book had scenes of Japanese or German forces attacking our troops or ships, and by covering these evil scenes we were taking an active role in the war."[18]

By 1944, Joe believes living in a 'foreign' land had become too much for Pappy, and they returned to their Fairview mountain-home. Since they had rented out their home while they were in Newport News, they had to move in with Pappy's sister, Marguerite, until the renters moved from their house. They lived there for about a year until the renters finally

---

[17] Douglas Brinkley, *The World War II Desk Reference*, (New York: HarperCollins, 2004), 388.

[18] Alexander, *The Forties* oral history.

vacated. They were back in their home by the time the war ended in 1945. Joe recalls when his brother, Bruce, and he held a victory celebration in their front yard after the radio announcement that the war was finally over. He remembers wishing they had fireworks, but they made do with beating on pans and tubs. Celebrations throughout Appalachia were widespread and numerous, many people reveling with whatever meager ways they had. By the end of World War II, Appalachia had undergone drastic changes during the region's history. In addition to the tremendous changes wrought by the Great Depression and then World War II, the enormous outmigration and changes to Appalachia's economy forever impacted the region.

Joe concludes his story, stating the Alexander's journey through the 1940s had come to an end. Appalachians had proven their strength and resilience in enduring life on the home front. Rachel Dunaway Cox, in "Can Families Take It?" states, "The social forces buffeting American families were undeniably powerful. Although family life was severely tested, the American family showed its resilience time after time in the face of dislocation, separation, and even death." Cox continues, "As much as the war battered mothers, fathers, and children, it also deepened their appreciation of family togetherness."[19] Many Appalachians had migrated during the

---

[19] Rachel Dunaway Cox, *Can Families Take It?,* quoted in Marilyn M. Harper, *World War II & the American Home Front: A*

war to find employment and had remained in their new homes. For others, being away deepened their appreciation of their homelands. They were willing to live elsewhere according to economic needs, but once that was no longer necessary, many returned and put an end to their homesickness. Joe professes a permanent move could never have been their fate, stating there was an influence for their family that never weakened or waned through those times, or any other. "It was a force that could not be denied and one that had to be accepted and accommodated. It severely limited the time we could be away from the mountains. Pappy's mountains demanded our presence."[20]

National Historic Landmarks Theme Study, (Washington, D.C.: Department of the Interior, 2007), 71.

[20] Alexander, *The Forties* oral history.

BIBLIOGRAPHY

Alexander, Joseph Richard, interview by Diane Alexander. The
     Forties (August 2008).
Alexander, Roy. Power Speech: The Quickest Route to
     Business and Personal Success. New York:
     AMACOM, Division of American Management
     Association, 1986.
Brinkley, Douglas. The World War II Desk Reference. New
     York: HarperCollins, 2004.
Cox, Rachel Dunaway. "Can Families Take It?" In World War
     II and the American Home Front, by Marilyn Harper.
     Washington, D. C.: U.S. Deparment of the Interior, The
     National Historic Landmarks Program, 2007.
Elder, Jr., Glen H. . "Social History and Life Experience." In
     World War II and the American Home Front, by
     Marilyn Harper. Washington, D.C.: U.S. Deparment of
     the Interior, The National Historic Landmarks Program,
     2007.
Eller, Ronald D. Uneven Ground: Appalachia Since 1945.
     Lexington: University Press of Kentucky, 2009.
Evans-Hylton, Patrick. Hampton Roads: The World War II
     Years. Mount Pleasant: Arcadia Publishing, 2005.
Fox, William A. Downtown Newport News. Mount Pleasant:
     Arcadia Publishing, 2010.
Harper, Marilyn M. World War II & the American Home
     Front: A National Historic Landmarks Theme Study.
     Washington, D.C.: National Historic Landmarks
     Program, 2007.
Panchyk, Richard. World War II for Kids: A History. Chicago:
     Chicago Review Press, 2002.
Wolf, Anna W.M., and Irma Simonton Black. "What
     Happened to the Younger People." In World War II and
     the American Home Front, by Marilyn Harper.
     Washington, D.C.: U.S. Deparment of the Interior, The
     National Historic Landmarks Program, 2007.

Firewood

Joseph Alexander

Modern folk probably think of firewood as an optional item that you may want or not. Those who don't have a fireplace probably don't think of firewood at all. It was not like that at our house. We relied on wood for heating, cooking and water heating. This meant that we had to keep a fire in the kitchen stove, a Home Comfort, every day regardless of the outside temperature. This was okay in the winter but on hot summer days the temperature in the kitchen and house reached very uncomfortable levels, and summer was the time of year for canning. Sometimes Buh would can vegetables or fruit from daylight to dusk in a kitchen that grew hotter as the day wore on. I tried to avoid the kitchen on those days and it was better to be entirely out of the house. Our home required a lot of firewood. So how does a family procure and process this rather large wood requirement for a Fairview household like ours? Some do better at this task than we did. Had there been a Fairview firewood procurement oversight committee, I'm sure our firewood system would have been graded poor to abysmal - minus.

The centuries-old tried and proven method for laying in wood for winter was to cut the wood in the <u>summer</u>. After allowing it to season (dry) for a time, the wood would be re-cut and spit to usable lengths, then stacked and covered and allowed to dry further until it was needed in the fall. This would produce firewood (almost always oak, ash and hickory) that would burn slowly, produce a great amount of heat, smoke little, produce very small amounts of creosote that could cause a chimney fire, and would usually preclude the need to cut wood in the cold days of winter. For whatever reason, we did not buy into this plan. WE CUT FIREWOOD WHEN WE NEEDED FIREWOOD.

Lest it be thought that wood gathering mirrors that of King Wenceslas in medieval times where it seemed possible, according to the carol, to wander out in the snow and gather fuel for the fire, you need to know more about the wood cutting process. More in particular, you might need to know more about The Alexander Wood Procurement Method. The Alexander process started by locating a hickory, ash or oak tree, not too big but big enough to produce a reasonable quantity of firewood, and then make sure the tree was accessible to the wood crew. That would be me and Pappy most of time. Looking back, I don't remember Bruce taking part in the tree downing process but he must have been a participant at some time. Roy had already flown the coop and would have had little or no interest in wood cutting had he been there. I didn't either, but I was "it". The selected tree also had to be in a location that could be reached by the Ferguson tractor and trailer. The immediate area around the tree had to be cleared so the saw crew would be able to work the crosscut saw. I have to stop here and tell you about the saw.

The crosscut saw was a marvelous tool! It felled millions upon millions of trees and provided lumber and wood products for a fledgling, wood-hungry republic. The principle of the crosscut saw is simple. The blade (very sharp) has a handle on each end so two men can join in the cutting process. One pulled the cutting blade through the wood and then the man on the other end pulled the blade back through the wood being cut. If there had been a crosscut instruction manual it would have cautioned the users that under no circumstances should either logger PUSH on the blade. The manual might have had Pappy in mind with this instruction. He seemed to always think the other end of the saw was not being pulled fast enough. The manual would have gone on to say that if you did push on the blade, the saw could be "kinked". This meant that the blade had a crook in it and this curve in the blade would greatly increase the amount of pulling pressure required by the participants. Our saw had multiple kinks in it. It also was very dull because we had experimented with different tooth lengths and guessed wrong. It would take us about an hour to bring down a medium sized tree (16 to 18 inches in diameter). Since we usually only cut wood in the winter, the saw provided a good warming exercise on a cold day so there _were_ benefits to our plan. I guess that may be the only benefit of winter wood cutting that I can think of. A _good_ crew with a _good_ saw could have brought the tree down in half the time or less but we were handicapped in our work. Our handicaps were: I didn't have the strength or stamina to pull on the kinked saw for a half-hour without stopping and Pappy would have to stop to repack and relight his pipe. As one who has smoked a pipe, it amazes me that he could smoke all the time he was doing whatever he was doing. I never got that good at pipe smoking.

Once the tree was on the ground, we would have to trim and pull away all the limbs of the tree that were too small for firewood. This would take another hour at least. Then we would cut the tree into five-foot lengths with the crosscut saw. For a medium tree this might take a couple of hours. Now the lengths had to be split into a size that would fit into our stove. Interestingly, what looks like a stove-sized piece of wood out in the wild might turn out to be entirely too big for our stove or probably any other stove. We used a simple test for size. If it looked like it <u>might</u> fit in some stove, we didn't split it any more. The splitting was done with a "go-devil" and two wedges. The go-devil was a sledge hammer with a dull cutting edge on the back. The wedges were made of steel and about 14 inches long. The theory was to drive one wedge into the log and then follow it with the second wedge which would then release the pressure on the first wedge allowing it to be moved ahead of the second one. This plan didn't always work and when you had both wedges stuck in the wood, you wished that you might have a third wedge to free one or both of the stuck wedges. We didn't have a third wedge.

When the splitting was finished, we brought up the tractor and trailer and loaded the wood to be taken to our back yard firewood processing center. The "center" contained remnants of past wood operations such as sawdust, chips, bark and a "cut-off saw". The cut-off saw had been built out of scrap lumber, a pulley, an axle on some bearings and a very dull saw blade of about 24" diameter. The wood was stacked next to the saw awaiting the next wood processing stage. We had now spent a very full day and we felt well justified in leaving to tomorrow that which we never wanted to do today.

The wood would stay in the back yard processing center until a member of the household would announce that she could no longer cook nor provide hot water nor heat the home without wood. This would usually initiate a flurry of wood processing activities. The tractor would be fitted with a large pulley on its power take-off. Then we would drag out a continuous belt (probably eight inches wide and fifteen feet long), put it on the cut-off saw pulley, put it on the tractor pulley and work at the MIT solution to getting all three lined up with sufficient tension to run the saw. On the first tries, the belt would invariably run off one or both of the pulleys and the process would have to be restarted. When all was working and the dull blade was screaming like a banshee, Pappy would pick up the first five-foot section of split wood and place it on the wobbly trough that moved past the saw. My job was to grab the SHORT END AS IT WAS BEING CUT and hold it in such a manner that the blade would not bind. If I failed, I was told, the saw might implode spreading its teeth and mayhem throughout the community. It was usually at this time in the process that I realized there was no way we could ever get these huge chunks of wood in our heater stove, much less the kitchen stove which, oddly enough, required even smaller stove wood. Pappy said we would save the big chunks for the fireplace at Christmas but I thought we might need a bigger fireplace. When Christmas approached, sure enough, we would bring in these huge chunks of unsplit wood and muscle them into the living room fireplace. Sometimes it would take several days of building fire around these behemoths to get them to start burning. Then they might burn too much and, as there is really no way to control the fire in a fireplace, we would have to move around the house according to the temperature of the Christmas fire in the fireplace. I always looked forward to opening the living room for Christmas. At other times in the winter, the living room was closed off as were all the bedrooms. This was to conserve firewood. I guess we might have been the first save-the-trees folk.

Back to lumberjacking. When the five-foot lengths had been cut, the tractor was unhooked and returned to other duties. The cut-off stayed right there because it was hooked to the ground with stakes. It never occurred to me that other folk did not have to walk around a cut-off saw to get in their homes.

Now once again we had firewood. However it was GREEN firewood. It was essentially fireproof. In the space heater, the wood would smolder and sizzle and smoke. To get it to even do this you had to put dry wood around it to heat it up. We burned every scrap of wood/lumber on the place just trying to get our green wood to burn. Finally, the wood would lose some of its sap and would grudgingly burn. Then it was time to start the process over with the next chunk of green wood. Since all the wood had been cut and split to barely fit in the space heater, there was no wood for the cook stove yet. Ideally, to fire a kitchen cook stove you need uniform firewood sticks, in both length and cross-section, of seasoned wood with a complement of small, dry materials that could be used to control the temperature of the stove. Of the five basic cook stove requirements, we were lucky if we met one and I'm sure we met none most of the time. Buh would point this out to the wood crew but somehow our system never changed. The job of transforming oversized green heater wood to green stove wood was assigned to Bruce and me as Pappy had now met all of his responsibilities in the project. Bruce was older and "stronger" so he chose to be the splitter of the stove wood. That left me with the on-going task of seeing that the wood boxes in the house were always full of both kinds of firewood. As soon as Bruce split what he judged to be an ample amount of Home Comfort wood, then his responsibility was also over and he would disappear somewhere. As our hot water was supplied by the kitchen cook stove, the quality of the stove wood related directly to our bath schedules. Before anyone took a bath, they would go to the kitchen and check the amount of hot water (or lack thereof) by running their hand down the side of the hot water tank until the tank wall turned cool. We got very good at estimating how much hot water was in the tank. If there was not enough water, there were no baths.

Buh was never happy with the quality of our wood for good reason - our wood was pathetic. I remember many times when she would struggle mightily with the fire in the Home Comfort. If the wood was too large, she would have little room to put any small material around it. I remember trying to help with the fire and watch the sap running out of the end of the wood and knowing that all I could do would not be enough to get the fire going. Buh must have felt frustrated with the perpetual expectation that she make biscuits every day while having only large, green stove wood to accomplish this task.

When the war ended, there began some discussions about replacing the Home Comfort with an electric stove, but Pappy argued that the biscuits would never taste like Home Comfort biscuits. I think he even went so far as to threaten not to eat any biscuits cooked in an electric stove. This later proved to be an idle threat. Home appliances had started to become available and the discussion of an electric stove came up with more regularity. Somehow, Buh finally won this campaign and with great excitement, we watched as a new Frigidaire electric stove, a Frigidaire refrigerator, and a Judd Whitehouse water heater were delivered by an Asheville appliance store that advertised buying on time. I think I was more excited about the refrigerator than the other appliances because, until that time, we had no way to keep foods cold and the prospect of having cold drinks, ice, and maybe even ice cream was a luxury I could hardly believe.

The stove went into service. The refrigerator cooled our food. The water heater made hot water all the time instead of being dependent on a successful Home Comfort fire that day. That's when we discovered the home had a deficiency that had not been apparent before we plugged in our new devices. There was not enough electricity coming into the house to power all our new and wonderful appliances. The house had been wired many years before on the premise that the only use anyone would ever have of electricity would be for lighting. We had exceeded that projection when we hooked up the first appliance. The first clue that something might be amiss was the blown fuses. With our advanced knowledge of electricity we knew exactly what needed to be done. Bigger fuses. Then yet bigger fuses. When we reached the bigger fuse limit, Pappy found an electrician acquaintance who agreed to look at our problem. Though nothing was said to the family, I suspect that the electrician probably was amazed that our house had not burned to the ground. The electrician installed a make-do wiring that somehow powered our appliances most of the time with only sporadic fuse burn-outs, but we were still operating on the very edge of electrical collapse. This became apparent years later when we got our first TV. We found that the snowy, one channel picture went to the size of a postage stamp when Buh ran the oven to make Pappy's biscuits.

Now we had a cook stove and a water heater. No more stove wood was required. But - we still needed heater wood. Pappy then decided that the food stove, which was by far the most important, needed no wood so the heater wood was given an even lower priority than before. The lower priority also might have come from his defeat in his argument to keep the Home Comfort. For whatever reason, now even less wood was cut and still none in the summer. This lack of wood came to a crisis level in late fall or early winter one year after we had upgraded to electric appliances. No wood had been cut for the season and we had burned everything we could find that was flammable. Buh had had enough. Her admonitions hadn't worked. Her threats hadn't worked and she was COLD! Somewhere, she found an old coal grate that was used in a fireplace to burn coal and she brought this into our closed-off living room. She installed the grate in our living room fireplace which had not been used since the previous Christmas. She then found a place to buy coal and it was delivered to our back yard and dumped next to, or maybe on, the idle cut-off saw still staked firmly to the ground. Buh hauled a bucket of coal to her new quarters, filled the grate, lit it, and was warm for the first time that fall. She closed the door from the living room into the rest of the house and made no effort to make biscuits or any other food item in the kitchen. If fact, she ignored the kitchen entirely. When Pappy came in from the fields, the first thing he noticed was the pile of coal on or against his cut-off saw. Mystified, he went into the back door of the house leading into the kitchen to discover no smells of food cooking. His next surprise might have been the closed door into the living room which now seemed to be warm instead of icy cold as usual. Buh had set up her quarters and no invitations had been extended to others in the home. From that time on, I don't remember a time when we had no firewood at all. I do know that the quality (green vs. seasoned) did not change. Years later (after I left home) an oil furnace was installed in the home and this event probably brought an end to the perpetual battle of wills over firewood, though I've always wondered if there was complete agreement on the thermostat settings. The basis of the original argument was as simple as it was unresolvable: "I'm cold" versus "I'm not."

Spotlight on Appalachia: Settlers and Speech, Music and Moonshine

Diane Alexander

Table of Contents

Introduction

A spirit of innovation is generally the result of a selfish temper and confined views. People will not look forward to posterity, who never look backward to their ancestors.

~ Edmund Burke

Edmund Burke believed that without looking backward, people can never look forward. Many new cultural historians would agree. New cultural history, with its infusion of oral histories and genealogical family histories, highlights the progression from scientific methodology, to new social history, and on to new cultural history. This newer methodology, with its focus on people, their cultural identity, and understanding of their world and their roots before them, emphasizes how people have consciously shaped their lives rather than their lives being shaped by the past.

There is perhaps no more exemplar society than Appalachia that illustrates this progression. Appalachia has fought harder than most other American cultures in establishing an evenhanded reputation, dispelling various stereotypes such as being the land of hillbilly backwardness with a culture of harsh poverty and illiteracy that has entrapped its people, and enriching and preserving its heritage. Scholars who supported the poverty-stricken image of the Appalachians claimed their research revealed an oppressive culture that imprisoned its people. In contrast oral histories from Appalachia demonstrate that the people made their culture; the culture did not make the people.

Scientific and social science based writings and research are juxtaposed with Appalachian stories, histories and defenses, which assert that here was not a land that made the people and that did not sentence its people to a life of desolation and despair. In late twentieth century, noticeably since the 1980s, new cultural historians began emphasizing everyday people in their everyday lives and historiography began to have a new vision in Appalachia. Although the claim of oppressiveness and backwardness has been fought against since the early days of the region, new cultural history gave more merit and strength to the Appalachian voice. These new accounts work not only to lend support to the pioneer and patriotic spirit of her people, but dispel myths that this society was somehow abnormal, backward or oppressive. Oral histories, such as those of William Roy Alexander and Martha Ruth Upshaw Alexander, help illustrate how everyday Appalachian residents made their culture, with more choices and free will than is frequently seen in earlier studies and interpretation of the region.

Historical methods

Studies and research on Appalachia from scientific historians as early as the 1800s, and then social historians around mid-century twentieth century, have often not reviewed this region favorably. These historians' interpretations and critiques contain phrases such as "illiterate," "backward," and "unintelligent"; and offer views such as determinism that the land and isolation imprisoned Appalachians or that of a culture living in the present with age-old customs and beliefs. New cultural history employs aspects such as cultural identity, linguistics, oral histories, sociology and anthropology in its methodology, in addition to shifting the focus from class structure and "major players," to the common people and how they viewed their lives. In "The Appalachian Image Reexamined: An Oral History View of Eastern Kentucky"

(1983), Terry Birdwhistell and Susan Allen write, "And, as Appalachians themselves have increasingly written and spoken about their native land and people, a more balanced view of the mountain character has begun to replace former stereotypes. Oral history has opened avenues of communication which constantly reveal unsuspected truths about a people who have been generalized about to the point of caricature."[1]

It is the intent of this paper to illustrate the importance of new cultural history and its methodologies, utilizing genealogical family stories and oral histories of two lifetime residents of Buncombe County, along with other Appalachian oral histories, in better interpreting and bringing to light how people define their lives, create their culture and understand their universe and historical pasts.

Historiography

Appalachian culture is a topic that provides such entities as Hollywood, authors, historians, and sociologists with a wealth of material. The topic also seems to surface in cycles; a plethora of analytic influx followed by periods of silence. Interestingly, these cycles parallel the adoptions of new historiographical methodologies. Prolific writings on

---

[1] Terry Birdwhistell and Susan Emily Allen, "The Appalachian Image Reexamined: An Oral History View of Eastern Kentucky," *The Register of the Kentucky Historical Society* 81, no. 3 (1983): 288.

Appalachia appeared in the late 1800s, peaking again around the 1940s, and then resurging in the 1980s onward, bringing with it the adaptation of new cultural historiography.

Appalachia underscores different methodologies and mindsets employed in these various eras. Historians engaging the scientific methodology often conducted their research and structured their writings along one correct "scholarly" version of history, supported by scientific studies. Their subjects tend to be marginalized within history, often portrayed as pawns trapped by their society or class. Ellen Semple, in her *The Anglo-Saxons of the Kentucky Mountains: A Study in Anthropogeography* (1901), and John Fiske, in his *Old Virginia and Her Neighbors* (1897), are examples of historical interpretations from this era. Semple, an American geographer from Kentucky and a pioneer in anthropological studies of Appalachia, was a social determinist who theorized that Appalachians were prisoners of their environment. In her paper she writes, "The whole civilization of Kentucky mountains is so eloquent to the anthropogeographer of the influence of the physical environment, for nowhere else in modern times has the progressive Anglo-Saxon race been so long and so completely subjected to retarding conditions; and at no other time could the ensuing result present so startling a contrast to the achievement of the race elsewhere as in this progressive twentieth century."[2]

In Anthony Harkin's *Hillbilly: A Cultural History of an American Icon,* he writes of an article written in 1882 by an unsigned author detailing a trip to eastern Kentucky. The author wrote that his journey "presented shockingly backward people, 'who plough with a stick and fight with a club, think the earth to be flat and their ancestors gods…who, in many cases, neither read nor write…and who often can barely count to ten.'" The author concluded his article with, "…the no-account people, the 'poor white trash.'"[3] Harkins demonstrates how John Fiske's theories lent support to authors such as these by, "asserting that the southern backcountry was settled by paupers and petty criminals forced to the margins of civilization by the power of the tidewater slaveholding aristocracy and their own degenerate heredity," to which Fiske concluded "[t]here can be little doubt that the white freedmen of degraded type were the progenitors of a considerable portion of what is often called the 'white trash' of the South."[4]

New social historians began incorporating women, African Americans and Native Americans into the Appalachian mixture, for the first time revealing many aspects of ethnic culture previously unearthed or minimally studied.

---

[2] John B. Rehder, *Appalachian Folkways* (Baltimore: JHU Press, 2004), 19.

[3] Anthony Harkins, *Hillbilly: A Cultural History of an American Icon* (New York, NY: Oxford University Press, 2005), 42.

[4] Harkins, *Hillbilly*, 42.

Notwithstanding the beneficial addition of new disciplines and mindsets, there remained a demarcation line in Appalachia, often drawn along the lines of racial and ethnic classes. This era highlighted the social reformers, who while attempting to uplift this culture of people, in turn augmented the stereotype. These social historians, such as John C. Campbell and William Frost felt cultural revivals and uplifting of these "helpless souls" was necessary to forward the progress of the region. During this era of historical methodology there were increasing voices from the Appalachian people themselves, but seemingly not enough to outweigh these "redeemers of society."

Kai Erikson, a sociologist, Yale faculty member, and former president of the American Sociological Association, refers to "Old Appalachia" in his *Everything in Its Path: Destruction of Community in the Buffalo Creek Flood* (1978) as a "life of monotony and quiet…of isolation and self-sufficiency…of sorrow, yet it was borne of dignity and pride…a life that forever asked people to choose between resigning themselves to the futility of it all or rising up to collar the devil himself."[5] John C. Campbell, a pioneer in Appalachian studies, wrote the *Southern Highlander and His Homeland,* published in 1921. Campbell was a theologian and missionary who traveled extensively throughout the southern

---

[5] Kai Erikson, *Everything in Its Path: Destruction of Community in the Buffalo Creek Flood* (New York: Simon & Schuster, 1978), 71-72.

Appalachians. [6] He studied Scot-Irish settlers in the region, along with his wife Olive Dame Campbell, detailing these peoples' histories, ancestry, religions, social life and customs.[7] Campbell's work was one of the most in-depth and earliest studies of this region's peoples. Despite his extensive research, several have critiqued his claim that these Southern Highlanders were a homogenous group.

New cultural historians began concentrating on the history of culture itself. Dwight Billings, in his "Culture and Poverty in Appalachia: A Theoretical Discussion and Empirical Analysis," (1974) analyzes the impact and harm of the stereotyped Appalachian culture portrayed by his peers and predecessors. Billings examines the works of numerous historians, sociologist, and psychologists (not an inclusive list)

---

[6] John Charles Campbell, *The Southern Highlander and His Homeland* (New York: The Russell Sage Foundation, 1921), xi-xvi.

[7] The term Scot-Irish (alternatively Scots-Irish) has been debated, often favorably, to be a more accurate terminology for this particular group of people than Scotch-Irish; however numerous debates over the correct term still persist. The term Scotch-Irish is an Americanized term, not developed to describe the blending of two nationalities as the term hints, but rather was used to describe settlers from the Ulster region of Ireland (primarily to Virginia and North Carolina) and their religious views held in common by this group (largely Presbyterian) to distinguish them from other religious cultures. While either term is considered correct, the author believes regardless of whether discussing the migratory group from Ireland or a blend of nationalities, that a person from Scotland would not be called a "Scotch" but rather a Scot or Scots.

and details their research methodology, showing how some of their variables, data, and results can be proved faulty.[8] Laurel Shackelford in *Our Appalachia* (1988) presents a similar thesis in proclaiming that the so-called sociological studies performed by "in and out" visitors have created "bad sociology" which in turn creates "bad history."[9] Both Billings and Shackelford proclaim it imperative to dispel the myth of the "hillbilly mountaineer," as it is not merely the stereotyping itself that is harmful, but it actually hinders progress in the region. Additionally both authors profess the need for a solid and accurate sociological study that not only would present a more accurate history but would produce other benefits, such as highlighting the origins of many American cultural icons and features, as well as furthering the progress of the region.[10]

John Alexander Williams in *Appalachia: A History* (2001) agrees with Billings and Shackelford. He takes it a step further, proclaiming that notwithstanding Campbell's in-depth and sensitive study, Campbell and others in similar roles had, in actuality, amplified the stereotype of Appalachian. Billings

---

[8] Dwight Billings, "Culture and Poverty in Appalachia: A Theoretical Discussion and Empirical Analysis," *Social Forces* 53, no. 2 (December 1974): 315-323.

[9] Laurel Shackelford, *Our Appalachia: An Oral History*, ed. Bill Weinberg and Laurel Shackelford (University Press of Kentucky, reprint, 1988), 12.

[10] Billings, "Culture and Poverty in Appalachia," 322; Shackelford, *Our Appalachia*, 3-13.

asserts that the area was indeed not homogenous as Campbell claimed, and Williams agrees. Williams further proclaims that Campbell and others (such as Cecil Sharp) increased Appalachian myths by their "habit of generalizing about the entire southern Appalachian region, regardless of the geographic limits of a given investigator's research...by valuing it [Appalachia] in relation to its usefulness in advancing other projects...and finally by their tendency in [representing] Appalachia [as its] whiteness."[11] Margaret Anderson in her "Education in Appalachia: Past Failures and Future Prospects" (1964) discusses how Appalachia fought to preserve tradition while working to improve the educational system. Tom Brown in "Sugar in the Gourd: Preserving Appalachian Traditions" (1983) touches upon the same drive to protect tradition in both the educational system and in Appalachia's music. Other new cultural historiographies include accounts such as Terry L. Birdwhistell's and Susan Emily Allen's, who discuss the rediscovery of Appalachia in their article. They explain how oral histories have brought to light understanding of Appalachia's past, its stereotype, and the richness of voluminous information yet to be brought into its spotlight. It is their hope, along with many other new cultural historians, that the acceptance of oral histories and their acceptance into mainstream historical interpretations will

---

[11] John Alexander Williams, *Appalachia: A History* (University of North Carolina Press, 2001), 211.

reveal a region rich in her history and undeserving of the often cruel stereotype.[12]

Appalachian culture has been highly praised and has suffered brutal criticism as well. Appalachian society is arguably not a singular entity. That statement, in itself, illustrates why such varied material and opinion prevail. New cultural historians support their findings, and subsequently their theses, with the opinion that in the Appalachians, many different cultures have compiled to form unique regions; and within these regions there are as many differences as there are similarities. It is this focal point that seems to cause the most amount of debate. Historians, authors and sociologists who have considered the entire Appalachian region as a solitary, homogenous group have produced material in polar opposition to those who consider differing cultures and various aspects of this southern United States region. New cultural history lends support to the importance of these interpretations of these varied cultures and diverse Appalachian life.

---

[12] Billings, "Culture and Poverty in Appalachia," 315; Margaret Anderson, "Education in Appalachia: Past Failures and Future Prospects," *Journal of Marriage and Family* 26, no. 4 (November 1964): 443-446; Tom Brown, "Sugar in the Gourd: Preserving Appalachian Traditions," *Music Educators Journal* 70, no. 3 (November 1983): 52-55; Birdwhistell and Allen, "The Appalachian Image Reexamined," 302.

How did Appalachian culture begin and develop into its unique culture? According to the Appalachian Regional Commission, Appalachia's region consists of a 205,000 square mile area from northeastern Mississippi to southwestern and southern New York; with Southern Appalachia encompassing northern Georgia to West Virginia.[13] Historians frequently refer to Appalachia's "otherness"; in large part due to its isolation and distinctive features. Persons such as Semple and Fiske refer to a land and environment that hemmed the people in and deem that the reason for the region's purported backwardness. Semple claimed the retarding conditions of the environment in turn caused an underdeveloped society, while Fiske asserted that the region was settled by criminals and the poor, forced into the area from more northern areas by plantation slave owners.[14] B.H. Luebke and John Fraser Hart, in their journal article, "Migration from a Southern Appalachian Community," speak of hindering conditions in the Appalachian region, stating, "The deep conservatism which leads mountain people to choose to remain in an area which

---

[13] ARC: Appalachian Regional Commission, "Appalachian Region," http://www.arc.gov/index.jsp (accessed December 7, 2009).

[14] Katie Algeo, "Locals on Local Color: Imagining Identity in Appalachia," *Southern Cultures* 9, no. 4 (Winter 2003): 33; Harkins, *Hillbilly*, 42.

many of them freely admit is economically, socially, and culturally retarded…The Southern Appalachian farmer has something of the peasant's love of his land.[15]

Interestingly, they treat the mountaineers' sentiment toward land as solely a restriction to outward migration, while cursorily dismissing the love of the land and the peoples' preferences to stay where their ancestors settled centuries before. They speak of the choices to remain in the area as somewhat aberrant behavior of the people; and disparagingly state that if (only) the resident was to move he could become "an integrated and valuable citizen of his new urban community," going on to issue a patronizing caveat, "but he frequently requires assistance."[16]

Countless accounts, including family, regional, and national histories, demonstrate the desirability of and deliberateness in selecting this new home by many. In 1777, a treaty between North Carolina and the Cherokee Indians opened up new lands for settlement to the west of the former territory boundaries at Old Fort, North Carolina.[17] Immigrants into this region were predominantly agrarian and consisted largely of Scottish, Irish, German, and Dutch. Some settlers

---

[15] B.H. Luebke and John Fraser Hart, "Migration from a Southern Appalachian Community," *Land Economics* 34, no. 1 (February 1958), 48.

[16] Luebke and Hart, "Migration from a Southern Appalachian Community," 53.

[17] Campbell, *The Southern Highlander*, 66.

migrated from the colonies of Virginia, Maryland, and Pennsylvania; and others migrated directly from Europe. Settlers from northern American colonies migrated in search of benefits such as more desirable political, religious, and agricultural conditions. Primogeniture was a compelling factor for European migration. In addition to farming the expansive lands, even the poor could own land as well. Extensive arable lands allowed for the development of these settlers' primary occupations of farming and raising livestock. Persons of Scottish and Irish heritage found the region reminiscent of their homelands. In addition to the physical characteristics, the land shared many more similarities such as economic, social, and climatic features with Scotland and Ireland. Here in Appalachia was land that bridged the gap between their old home and their new, with benefits not available to them in their homelands.

These large groups of settlers shared many commonalities that allowed them to not only retain many of their customs, but to exert great influence on the preservation and growth of their new hybrid cultures, created from a blend of their homelands and their new lands. In large part due to the isolated mountain regions, the area did not see as much varied integration with numerous other societies, as was common in more coastal and northern colonies. Even into the twentieth century, the mountainous lands have allowed for a certain degree of separateness and remoteness. These conditions have allowed Appalachia to develop into "otherness" to which she is so frequently referred.

William Roy Alexander (Roy) (1899-1988) lived his lifetime on land in Buncombe County, North Carolina, that had been in his family since the eighteenth century.[18] In 1777, the Alexanders, Davidsons, McDowells and Pattons were among the first settlers into the new land opened by the treaty. Alexander's paternal great-great grandfather, James Alexander, was a Revolutionary War veteran and a soldier in the Battle of King's Mountain. James was also a prominent figure in the founding of Buncombe County. He and Colonel William Davidson, Roy's maternal great-great-great grandfather, were present at the first Buncombe County Court session, held in Davidson's barn. James was one of the first justices of Buncombe County. Colonel William Davidson was also a Revolutionary War veteran, and it was at his house that Buncombe County was initially organized and court held. Roy's great-great grandfather John Merrill was also a pioneer settler in this region; the Merrills well known for being anti-British and Revolutionary War veterans. The Alexanders, Davidsons, and Merrills were predominantly farmers, present

---

[18] William Roy Alexander was known by his middle name, Roy. In sections involving his occupation, he is referred to as Roy. To almost all friends and family, he was known as Pappy; and in sections such as music, where the name Roy was rarely heard, he is referred to as Pappy.

in Buncombe County since its inception in 1792, having moved from Rowan County and among the first white settlers in that region as well.[19]

Martha Ruth Upshaw (Ruth) (1902-1997) lived her childhood in Villa Rica, Georgia, her great-great grandfather Daniel Candler having first migrated to western North Carolina.[20] Zachariah Candler, grandson of Daniel, was the progenitor of almost all the North Carolina Candlers. Both the Candlers and the Alexanders owned extensive tracts of land in the Biltmore region, and both families sold large portions of their farmlands to George Vanderbilt (from which he created Biltmore Estate.) The Alexanders remained primarily in Buncombe County for the next century, while many of the Candlers migrated to Georgia. Ruth's grandfather, William Beall Candler, was brother to the successful Candlers of the Atlanta area, including the Honorable Milton Anthony Candler, the Honorable Charles Murphy Candler, the Honorable John Slaughter Candler, Bishop Warren Akin Candler, and druggist, Asa Candler, the founder of the Coca-Cola Company.[21] Ruth's teaching career and fondness for

---

[19] Campbell, *The Southern Highlander*, 66; Foster Alexander Sondley, *Asheville and Buncombe County* (Asheville: The Citizen Company, 1922), 87,151.

[20] Martha Ruth Upshaw married William Roy Alexander. She went by her middle name, Ruth, throughout most of her life. However, she was better known as Buh by friends and family and was rarely called Ruth.

learning may well have been instilled by her educated ancestors, many of whom were patrons of their local educational systems.

The physical and intangible assets of land were, and continue to be, a strong sentiment among many Appalachians. It is common to hear about the draw to the land and the custom of keeping family lands generation after generation. As a common sentiment toward the land, a local potter is quoted in "Education in Appalachia: Past Failures and Future Prospects" as saying, "Oh, I could work in a Northern factory… [but] Nothing would ever be my own," which Margaret Anderson says, "may explain in part why many mountain migrants are never really happy in the far-off factories and yearn for the hills of home."[22] Roy Alexander's son, Joe, writes about a visit home he and Roy took in the 1940s. The Alexander family was temporarily living in Newport News, Virginia where Roy was employed at the shipyard during World War II. Joe wrote in his short story "The Forties," "I think this homesick trip may have triggered a permanent return to the mountains for the Alexander family." He concluded his piece about their move back home to Cane Creek, Fairview, North Carolina with, "Pappy's mountains demanded our presence."[23]

---

[21] Allen D. Candler, *Colonel William Candler of Georgia: His Ancestry and Progeny* (Atlanta: The Franklin Printing & Publishing Company, 1902), 24-25.

[22] Anderson, "Education in Appalachia," 443.

While there are a myriad of migration patterns and reasons in Appalachia, the prevalence of Scot-Irish place names, Celtic customs, and surnames indicate the Scottish and the Irish, especially, found this region most conducive to their new lives in America. Demographics, showing the largest groups of Scottish and Irish still remain concentrated in southern Appalachia, combine with oral histories that overwhelmingly talk of the land and "taking a piece of it no matter where you go," supporting the claim that people made Appalachia their home from choice. While many had opportunities and choices to leave the area – and did so either permanently or temporarily – many always considered Appalachia their home. Here was land where the first drop of blood was shed for the colonies' independence; where the Battle of King's Mountain turned the tide of the Revolutionary War; and where countless American cultural items and icons -- music, mountain crafts, timber products, NASCAR, Nobel Prize winners, and scientists -- to name but a few – have been born. Oral histories and family traditions supplement the history of this region; not supporting the claim of an oppressive land that hemmed its people in but rather a land her people have great love for and always consider their home, even if transplanted and only in spirit.

---

[23] Joseph Alexander, "The Forties," in *The Alexanders: Memoirs of a North Carolinian Family* (Rocklin: Alexact Genealogy, 2009), 5.

One factor that contributes to the Appalachian stereotype of illiteracy or unintelligence is the region's vernacular. While earlier historians accepted Appalachians' distinctive way of speaking at face value, more recent scholars have studied the unique Appalachian dialect in an attempt to ascertain its origins and dissect the underlying logic of its speech patterns. In this, Appalachian historians have followed the wider historical trend of giving attention to linguistics, which has had a notable impact on historical interpretation since the latter half of the twentieth century.[24]

For instance, one unusual grammar pattern found in Appalachian speech is a-prefixing, the prefacing of a verb with "a", commonly used in phrases such as "He's gone a-huntin'." Linguistic research suggests this is the predominant verb usage in Scottish Gaelic. In Scottish Gaelic "tha e a'togail an tighe" translates as "he is building a house," but literally translates as "he is at building a house" or "he is a-building a house."[25] Southern Appalachians were predominantly Scottish and Irish and many of their speech patterns naturally migrated with these settlers in the eighteenth century. Thus, Julia C. Dietrich, in her

[24] Martha Howell and Walter Prevenier, *From Reliable Sources: An Introduction to Historical Methods* (Ithaca: Cornell University Press, 2001), 88-89.

[25] Donnie Macdonald, Scottish Gaelic Lessons, notes taken by author, 2002.

journal article "The Gaelic Roots of A-Prefixing in Appalachian English," argues, "[The vernacular's] unique features result not from a careless handling of English grammar but from a careful preservation of Scottish Gaelic grammar, learned generations ago and applied to English long before the migration to America."[26]

Roy Alexander began studying dialect and speech patterns in his Appalachian community, which had a long-standing custom of oral tradition. In his book *Power Speech*, Alexander also supports the linguistic theory of Gaelic origin by stating, "through these oral traditions passed from generation to generation came speech that 'in many ways…echoed characteristics of Elizabethan English in its vocabulary, its grammar and, above all, its vitality – slangy, hasty, playful, and often insulting.'"[27]   Given its purported origin, it is not surprising that this verb usage is found among Alexander progenitors in western North Carolina, almost all of whom were Scottish or Irish.

---

[26] Julia C. Dietrich, "The Gaelic Roots of A-Prefixing in Appalachian English," *American* Speech 56, no. 4 (Winter 1981): 314. For further reading on Appalachian English see Walt Wolfram, "Mountain Speech: Sociolinguistic Factors and the Significance of Appalachian English" (speech, Cleveland State University, March 1976).

[27] Roy Alexander, *Power Speech: The Quickest Route to Business and Personal Success* (New York: AMACOM, Division of American Management Association, 1986), 3-5.

Other linguistic theorists concur with the Elizabethan origins of speech patterns; however, some of these scholars interpret the persistence of these patterns as evidence for cultural backwardness. In W.K. McNeil's *Appalachian Images in Folk and Popular Culture*, Ellen Semple is quoted, "In one of the most progressive and productive countries of the world…we find a large area where the people are still living the frontier life of the backwoods, where the civilization is that of the eighteenth century, where the people speak the English of Shakespeare's time...."[28] In *Appalachian Folkways*, John B. Rehder points out that others disagree entirely with the English origins. He details some of the common myths of Appalachian speech, such as, "One assumption is that since, to some, the speech sounds coarse, unsophisticated, and uncultured, it has no place in America and certainly could not have come from the proper speech patterns currently used in the British Isles."[29] Still others state the unique vernacular is born of illiteracy, lowbrow speech, and common among poorer classes of persons. Redher explains how John Fox Jr. in his "The Southern Mountaineer" (1901) was a "color writer who left an indelible mark on the image of Appalachia."[30] Fox interpreted

---

[28] W. K. McNeil, *Appalachian Images in Folk and Popular Culture*, ed. W. K. McNeil (UMI Research Press, 1989, Original from Indiana University), Google digitized book June 8, 2009, 146.

[29] Rehder, *Appalachian Folkways*, 289.

[30] Rehder, *Appalachian Folkways*, 27.

the cultural backwardness as offering no incentive to change, "An arrest of development follows; so that once imprisoned, a civilization, with its dress, speech, religion, customs, ideas, may be caught like the shapes of lower life in stone, and may tell the human story of a century as the rocks tell the story of an age."[31]

While there is validity in the distinction between low-brow and high-brow speech (e.g. Cockney vs. formal English diction) new cultural historians point out that this vernacular was not born of simply unintelligence or low class, but rather was part of cultural identity and preserved customs and traditions. There are as many distinct speech patterns as there are cultures in Appalachia, supporting the claim that the region is indeed not homogenous. What is important in discussing Appalachian dialect is the fact that her people have always retained the choice in their vernacular. Americans have sung along to numerous a-prefixed lyrics in songs such as Bob Dylan's "The Times They Are A-Changin'," Elvis Presley's "It Keeps Right on A-Hurtin'," and Manfred Mann's "There she was just a-walkin' down the street" in "Do Wah Diddy Diddy." While these lyrics are usually not found objectionable, when a Southerner says, "I'm going a-fishin'" with a southern drawl and at slower speed than many American dialects, the stereotype is augmented. The picking and choosing of

---

[31] Rehder, *Appalachian Folkways*, 27.

acceptable usage of grammar patterns such as a-prefixing makes it difficult to overcome the negative image, often unfairly placed, of Appalachian speech and its people.

In spite of their oral heritage, the Alexanders did not favor Appalachian speech patterns over proper English. This was especially true with Ruth and in the rearing of her children. Although Ruth spoke with a southern accent (a dialect choice), she was a school teacher and, judging from her memoirs, seemed very aware of how speech patterns foster the development of stereotypical perceptions toward Appalachians from outsiders. Her son, Roy Alexander, began interviewing her in the late 1980s, compiling her memoirs in "Memoirs in Chalkdust: My 31 Years as an Appalachian Schoolteacher." When Roy transcribed a section of the interview, he wrote "chirren" for "children," which was a common pronunciation in southern accent. When Ruth edited the transcript, she emphatically commented on this transcription, stating she might talk with a southern accent that tends to slur pronunciation, but she had never used the word "chirren" for children. There seemed to be some debate over this issue, as Roy included a humorous note in the transcript stating he changed it to "children" but wrote, "she says 'I don't say chirren; I say chirren.'"[32]

---

[32] Ruth Upshaw Alexander, *Memoirs in Chalkdust: My 31 Years as an Appalachian Schoolteacher*, Oral history interview by Roy Alexander and personal memoir, transcript, private collection

William and Ruth Alexander spoke with a southern drawl, albeit proper English the vast majority of the time. Regardless of their heritage and environment, they were not trapped by the inability to speak other than "hillbilly speech," that is, their Appalachian environment did not doom them to a life of illiteracy and improper English. Memoirs and oral histories, such as Ruth's, indicate that speech was, for the large part, a matter of personal preference and choice. Her memoirs also indicate she was aware of the ramifications of stereotyped Appalachian dialect. Great literary talents and Nobel Prize winners, including Thomas Wolfe, Pearl Buck, Henry Louis Gates, Annie Dillard, and Frances Hodgson Burnett additionally belie the claim that Appalachia's unique dialect imprisoned its people.

Music

In perhaps no other forum than Appalachian music is the progression of historical interpretation more vividly illustrated. One of the many contributions of Appalachian culture to American society has been its music. While there are few that dispute the contribution this cultural component has had upon modern American music, the degree of impact, the origins and even the quality of this music has been contested. This area, as with many others in the study of Appalachian

(1997-1998), 19-20.

culture, exemplifies the debate between experts about Appalachia's contributions and equitable reputation.

Around the turn of the twentieth century, the prime focus for many was locating and categorizing Appalachian music of Anglo-Saxon roots. These early musical studies were often interpreted with "scientific method," that is, based on archives and artifacts and comparable to the views of Leopold von Ranke (1795-1886): "if it is not in the documents, it does not exist."[33] Historians and music aficionados analyzed the roots of folk music, forming theories about its origins, lyric meanings, musical instruments, and musical notations such as shape notes. When collecting this music increased in popularity beginning in the late 1800s, Appalachia became an active region for locating many of the ballads that had journeyed across the ocean with early Americans.

One of the most widely acclaimed studies of Appalachian folk music is that of Cecil Sharp, who toured the Appalachian region in the early 1900s and collected folk songs. Cecil Sharp was a musician in England who began compiling ballads and scores of his country's songs, arising from a desire to keep the traditional music for posterity. A search for more music brought him to America in the early 1900s, where he found that in Appalachia many of the traditional songs had migrated with the people, albeit taking on new qualities in its

---

[33] Howell and Prevenier, *From Reliable* Sources, 12.

ocean journey. For all the acclamation Sharp's work received -- scholars would base their research on it for the next fifty years -- there was still much criticism. Some proclaimed he overtly ignored any origins to folk music other than what he deemed as having pure British roots, such as the influence of Negro spirituals and gospel, as well as the influence of other settlers in the region such as German, Swiss, French, Cajun, and Hispanic upon Appalachian music.[34] Sharp appeared to be more focused on the scientific method of studying the music, in order to bring ballads back to his homeland, than he was interested in the people from which he collected his songs, referring to the Southern Appalachians as a "lower race."[35] One of his primary beliefs as to why the music was better preserved in Appalachia than in any other region of America was due to the isolated region and purported free time mountaineers had.[36]

Appalachian musical interpretation began to shift focus around the turn of the twentieth century, picking up popularity

---

[34] Peggy Langrall, "Appalachian Folk Music: From Foothills to Footlights," *Music Educators Journal* 72, no. 7 (March 1986): 37-39.

[35] Jeff Biggers, *The United States of Appalachia: How Southern Mountaineers Brought Independence, Culture, and Enlightenment to America* (Emeryville: Shoemaker & Hoard, 2006), 12.

[36] Ann Ostendorf, "Song Catchers, Ballad Makers, and New Social Historians: The Historiography of Appalachian Music," *Tennessee Historical Quarterly*, 63 (Fall 2004): 193.

toward the 1930s and 1940s, as "social reformers" became involved in American societal aspects. John and Olive Dame Campbell, and Emma Bell Miles (*Spirit of the Mountain*), began as early as the 1900s, focusing on Appalachian music in its ability to uplift the people, while concurrently emphasizing the Anglo-Saxon roots and preserving its tradition. This era produced interesting interpretations upon the music, as social historians, whether intentionally or not, categorized Appalachian music emphasized along racial and class lines. While social historians accomplished things such as escalating the popularity of American music, and in part were responsible for a clearer demarcation of when America's music became her own rather than a product of European heritage, these accomplishments more so augmented the image of the supposed backward Appalachians.[37] Despite the Campbell's extensive missionary activities, their attempts at arts, crafts and music revivals were done "without respecting the ability to do so themselves [mountaineers]...."[38] The Roosevelts joined in the music revival of the 1930s and 1940s in the push to appreciate and enjoy America's art. According to Ann Ostendorf in her article, "Song Catchers, Ballad Makers, and New Social Historians," the Roosevelts "saw folk art as allowing those who might typically feel they had no voice in

---

[37] Ostendorf, "Song Catchers," 199.
[38] Ostendorf, "Song Catchers," 199.

government to believe they too contributed to the building of America."[39]

In the late twentieth century, particularly the 1980s onward, new cultural historians began focusing on the multiple cultures infused into Appalachia's music. Despite Sharp's contribution in compiling almost two thousand folk songs, he received criticism from others for both generalizing the Appalachian culture as a whole and ignoring the infusion of other cultures into Appalachian folk music. Bill C. Malone, author of *Southern Music/American Music* (2003), acknowledges Sharp's contribution to the region's cultural history, but similarly states that with the addition of other influence upon the music, including Black gospel and spiritual, German, Cajun, and Mexican, that not only did Sharp dismiss the impact these groups made, but moreover with the infusion of so many other genres and styles, determining the precise origins of Appalachian music could not be done, as Sharp professed to have done. Malone's overarching claim is that despite Sharp's good intentions, his research created a false impression of the region and its music that "scholars to date have still not overcome."[40] It is precisely debates such as this that targets the issue underlying the debate as to Appalachia's cultural contributions, reputation, and stereotypes.

---

[39] Ostendorf, "Song Catchers," 199.

[40] Bill C. Malone and David Stricklin, *Southern Music/American Music* (University of Kentucky Press, 2003), 32.

Malone explains that revising the book *Southern Music: American Music* was in large part due to the explosion of scholarly and popular writing responses after the book's initial release. He states, "The South has exerted a powerful influence on American music in two important ways: as a source of image and symbols, both positive and negative, which have fueled the imaginations of musicians and songwriters and as an incubus of entertainers and styles that have shaped the entire realm of American popular music."[41]

He goes on to affirm,

"Southerners turned naturally to music because it was an integral part of their cultural inheritance and because it provided a means of release and a form of self-expression that required neither power, status nor affluence...This musical transformation reflected and paralleled the South's rise in national prominence, a process in which a region became more like the country and the country became more like the South...the land that gave rise to virtually every form of American popular music."[42]

The Alexander family tradition of music fits the characteristics of southern music described by Malone: "cultural inheritance…a means of release…and a 'form of self-expression.'"[43] Their music rituals also resembled Tom

---

[41] Malone and Stricklin, *Southern Music/American Music*, 1.
[42] Malone and Stricklin, *Southern Music/American Music*, 3.
[43] Malone and Stricklin, *Southern Music/American Music*, 3.

Brown's descriptions in "Sugar in the Gourd: Preserving Appalachian Tradition," for instance, "a prominent part of Southern Mountain life…authentic folk musicians who are living links in oral tradition." Brown explains, "To this day, the Appalachian ear is partial to string music, and the ability to play a fiddle or pick a banjo is still held in high esteem in mountain communities."[44] It would be difficult to examine the Alexander family documents of pictures, personal letters, memoirs, and family heirlooms without recognizing that music was an integral cultural event for this family.

Joseph Alexander (Joe) begins his story "The Music," with "There was always music."[45] He writes, "We sang, we whistled, we hummed, and we played combs and spoons. It might have not been good music, but if we noticed any deficiencies, it didn't reduce our need for it. We had family music sessions with Buh playing her Gibson Junior mandolin and Pappy strumming his Kay guitar, and the rest of us trying to sing whatever was played."[46]

Joe writes that Pappy insisted that "old-time music" could only be heard in the mountains of North Carolina. During World War II, Buh and Pappy (William and Ruth

---

[44] Brown, "Sugar in the Gourd," 53, 55.

[45] Joseph Alexander, "The Music," in *The Alexanders: Memoirs of a North Carolinian Family* (Rocklin: Alexact Genealogy, 2009), 1.

[46] Alexander, "The Music," 1.

Alexander) moved to Newport News, Virginia with their sons. Pappy worked in the shipyard during wartime. Upon the Alexanders move back to Buncombe County, Pappy, having suffered withdrawals from what he considered authentic (and THE only) mountain music, began looking for musicians in the area for impromptu music sessions. Pappy recruited several musicians, beginning with his first lead through their mail carrier. Eventually there were enough musicians to gather at the Alexander home on Saturday nights, including the mail carrier, Red Dills, who was a mandolin player; a five-string banjo player Homer Israel; and a fiddler Johnny Miller.[47]

These music sessions of entertainment, relaxation, and camaraderie were not without ritual. Joe stated it would begin with the musicians' arrival, taking their seats and placing the instrument cases on the floor, proceeding to ignore their existence. Small talk would occur until Pappy would turn to someone and say something to the effect of, "Homer, how 'bout getting' that banjer outta the case and let me see it." One by one, the musicians would all participate in this ritual, until all the instruments were out of their case and the tuning process would then begin. Tuning instruments in Appalachian homes is not a rapid process; in fact, it is part of the performance. Joe states that there was an "ancient old-time musician's code" of never simply going into a song without

____

[47] Alexander, "The Music," 2.

endorsement and expressions of modesty. Pappy, for instance, would say, "Johnny, let's hear a little of that Cripple Creek." Johnny would protest and state he had not played that in ages and was not sure if he even remembered it, however Joe states after such an intro, a player would proceed to play the piece with perfection, belying the fact that the musician had not played that piece so long ago as to have forgotten it. However, humbleness was part of the music ritual, as well as being a predominant trait among many Appalachians.[48]

Similar to listening to a bard or storyteller whose story sweeps the audience along, this same process is seen in Appalachian music playing. The music would improve as the story built, and the musicians at the Alexander home would go through their repertoire, including many tunes "learned from their kin, who learned it from their kin, ad infinitum."[49] Despite the Alexander family being immersed deeply in this region's musical culture, social historians would likely have ignored their home in their search for music. The family did not seem to fit the mold of Appalachian music of only pure Anglo-Saxon roots; nor did they engage in music as an attempt to improve their social standing or circumstances. Impromptu musical gatherings in Appalachian homes, such as these, would give birth to one of the South's largest industry – music. A vast

---

[48] Alexander, "The Music," 3.
[49] Alexander, "The Music," 4.

portion of modern American music, including country, bluegrass, folk, and blues, has its roots in Appalachia.

Ruth Alexander wrote of her musical childhood in her memoirs, reminiscing that, "Almost always, when she [Mother] was doing her housework she was singing." She continues, "Father liked to tell us stories, [and] sing us songs…and if he got to the end of one, he'd go right on, making up more words, making wonderful stories out of them."[50] In *Our Appalachia,* Pearl Cornett speaks of her mother always singing. When Pearl asked of her mother if she ever got tired of singing, her mother replied, "Alas for those that who do not sing and die and take all their music with them."[51] Even Sharp, in either a decidedly uncritical remark or backhanded compliment, was quoted as saying, "They (mountaineers) have the advantage over those who habitually spend the greater part of every day in preparing to live, in acquiring the technique of life, rather than in its enjoyment."[52] In "Appalachian Music is Alive and Kicking," Martha Smith writes, "The mountain people have always had a gift for composing folk songs or improvising on old ballads they brought to the new land with them. Young people today value this part of their cultural heritage and are determined not to let

---

[50] Alexander, *Memoirs in Chalkdust,* 29-30.

[51] Shackelford, *Our Appalachia,* 315.

[52] Mack McCormick, "The Musical Resources of American Folklife," *Music Educators Journal* 56, no. 1 (September 1969): 49.

it disappear."[53] The infusion of banjos (thought to originate in Africa), the dulcimer with its Greek zither origins (and a musical instrument predominantly manufactured in the Appalachians), and the fiddle with its ancient European origins, combine in this genre of music, portraying a blend of multiple cultures and daily lives of so many Appalachian music makers.[54]

The music tradition in the Alexander home, like countless other Appalachian homes, was a vital component – a reward and relaxation after hard work, a social outlet, a reason to visit with neighbors and to share heritage and tradition. Frequently music was an educational tool; often with a moral or value intertwined with the lyrics. Appalachian music, like in the Alexander home, was certainly not representative of having too much time on one's hands or the need to uplift poverty-stricken souls. Rather it was an ingrained tradition, much like the intangible portion of land, in which the people reveled. It was their heritage, tradition, and mode of entertainment. Oral histories from this region speak volumes to the cultural life of Appalachians in aspects such as family values, standards, morals, personalities, daily lives, and customs.

---

[53] Martha Smith, "Appalachian Music is Alive and Kicking," *Appalachia* 6, no.1 (Sep 72): 26-33.

[54] Biggers, *The United States of Appalachia*, 13.

Moonshine

Hand in hand with the stereotypical poverty and hillbillies of Appalachia is the image of a moonshiner. Mass media including comic strips and television shows, as well as numerous historians and authors, have done much to promote the typical moonshiner as a bedraggled, toothless, poorly educated hillbilly living in a shack in the mountains and running from revenuers. Moonshine has a long-standing tradition in the Appalachians, predating Prohibition (notably the point at which criminal aspects of the whiskey industry entered the mix), dating to the Whiskey Rebellion in the eighteenth century. The Appalachian region was largely populated with Scot-Irish settlers, and whiskey making was not only a common and economic process, but for the most part born of familial traditions. Corn was a staple food product in the Appalachians; its many uses included corn meal, dolls, furniture seats, fire starter, and hog and cattle feed. According to Roy Alexander's foreword in "The Corn-Liquor Chase" farmers in the Appalachian region could not sell their surplus corn crop locally. By turning the crop product into alcohol, profits could now be realized in this crop. The equipment was simple; however, the skill levels in distillation varied greatly.[55]

---

[55] William Roy Alexander, *The Corn-Liquor Chase: Memoirs of a 1930s Appalachian Deputy Sheriff*, Oral history interview by Roy Alexander, private collection, 1985, 1-2; Williams,

In *Appalachia: A History,* John Williams states taxes had gone uncollected in Appalachia following the Whiskey Rebellion. In 1862, the taxes on alcohol (particularly whiskey and brandy) were reenacted as a source of wartime revenue, although it was not enforced until Rutherford B. Hayes became president in 1877. Hayes, a teetotaler, believed both the governmental positions created for revenue agents as well as the additional tax revenues would be beneficial for the United States. Williams posits post-Civil War ramifications entered the political aspects of moonshine at this time as well, "Enforcing revenue laws in the southern backcountry was a way of proclaiming federal supremacy in the South just as federal troops were being withdrawn from the region...."[56] Resistance to moonshining, and subsequent resultant violence, tended to follow economic signifiers. Farmers needed to distill moonshine in hard times to make ends meet, notably during the 1890s and during the Depression years of the 1930s, while they experienced more prosperity during the 1880s and 1920s.[57]

In Wilbur R. Miller's article, "The Revenue: Federal Law Enforcement in the Mountain South, 1870-1900," he talks of one reason for the escalation in the moonshine industry. By 1916 all the old moonshine states except Kentucky and Missouri were dry, and blockaders enjoyed a vastly expanded

---

Appalachia, 118; Miller, "The Revenue," 199.

[56] Williams, *Appalachia*, 187.

[57] Williams, *Appalachia*, 188.

market and unprecedented profits. Some people thought moonshiners favored prohibition because of the opportunities it offered them. Prohibitionists hoped to reform the community's morality; instead, they encouraged lawlessness and resentment of a bureaucratic state that had extended itself too deeply into citizens' lives… [I]f the moonshiner opposed modernization in the form of the revenuer, he took advantage of it for his own profit in the form of prohibition. Blockaders were strengthened not because of any weakness or loss of commitment by the federal government but because of the unintended support from fellow southerners, who thought they could enlist government to reform people's drinking habits.[58]

This mixture of moonshine tradition, politics, and agriculture would fuel a topic that would produce countless material for stories, studies, media, historians, authors, and Appalachia's history.

In "Locals on Local Color," Katie Algeo discusses Ellen Semple's descriptions of Appalachian society, including "ignorance, feuds, intoxication, and lawlessness."[59] Others like William Goodell Frost, president of Berea College in 1893, also contributed to the Appalachian stereotype. Frost, in spite

---

[58] Wilbur R. Miller, "The Revenue: Federal Law Enforcement in the Mountain South, 1870-1900," *The Journal of Southern History* 55, no. 2 (May 1989): 216.

[59] Algeo, "Locals on Local Color: Imagining Identity in Appalachia," 33.

of his assertions to assist the Appalachians, often augmented the stereotype. Before the Chautauqua Assembly in 1903, he offered a solution to the violence (i.e. feuding and moonshining) in Appalachia, "[T]he cure of the feud must lie in that moral progress which is called education… [W]e are proposing not merely to prevent the mountain people from being a menace, but to bring the people of Appalachian America over from the ranks of the doubtful classes and range them with those who are to be the patriotic leaders and helpers of the new age."[60] This so-called "Appalachian crisis" by many social historians reached its peak in the 1930s and 1940s. In the late 1940s, a park promoter from Virginia is quoted in *Appalachia: A History*, as arguing his cause "…by portraying the communities concerned as rife with illiteracy, immorality, inbreeding, moonshining, and lawlessness."[61] Williams asserts all these accusations have since been refuted; with the exception of moonshining having the only legitimate basis of truth.[62] Since the early days of revenue agent stories, critical descriptions of Appalachia people often depicted a violent and lawless land, involving almost barbaric people brewing and defending their goods in the southern mountains.

---

[60] Dwight B. Billings and Kathleen M. Blee, *The Road to Poverty: The Making of Wealth and Hardship in Appalachia* (Cambridge: Cambridge University Press, 2000), 311.

[61] Williams, *Appalachia*, 305.

[62] Williams, *Appalachia*, 305.

In various oral histories, including that of Roy Alexander's "The Corn-Liquor Chase" which details his experiences spent as a deputy sheriff in Buncombe County chasing bootleggers, the issue of moonshine can be seen in a different light than what many have been exposed to, for instance in media works such as the *Snuffy Smith* or *L'il Abner* comic strips, the *Beverly Hillbillies* or the *Dukes of Hazzard* television shows, or in studies by persons such as Semple and Frost. These oral histories add details to both a traditional and economic feature of Appalachian culture that, while having both inside supporters and critics, gives additional insight into the whiskey industry and its participants. Wilbur R. Miller writes in "The Revenue: Federal Law Enforcement in the Mountain South, 1870-1900," "Most mountaineers were not moonshiners. The minority who were practiced the complicated art of distillation with varying levels of skill and acted out of diverse motives ranging from economic necessity to the quest for profit."[63] The director of the Appalachian Center at Berea College, Gordon B. McKinney, (*Southern Mountain Republicans, 1863-1900: Politics and the Appalachian Community* 1978) offers that blockading was a "mountaineer adaptation to social change...the more enterprising secured capital and started their own business utilizing the resources of the mountains," and was an argument

---

[63] Miller, "The Revenue," 199.

against the inability claimed by others for Appalachians to not integrate and adapt to change.[64]

Roy Alexander began his moonshine deputy duties with the Buncombe County Sheriff's Department in 1930, by hunting stills on foot with a special deputy assigned solely to finding these stills. Riding and driving in automobiles were not tasks assigned to newly appointed deputies. Before learning to chase bootleggers, Roy claimed the deputy had to learn to ride; emphasizing many deputies failed this initial test. It took Roy three years to learn how to ride before he ever drove. Running at speeds of 80 mph with automobiles and roads of the 1930s is barely comparable to today's road driving. Because of the fact moonshine was predominantly produced in mountainous areas, the roads were rarely straight, broad, or driver-friendly. On mountain roads Roy described as "a shelf chopped out the mountainside," all passengers would have to shift to the inner side to keep the car upright. Even still, the cars would often go on two wheels during chases. It was a dangerous activity.[65] There were only a few deputies that could drive well enough to keep up with the runners; and in addition, it could get dangerous quickly if the moonshiner began shooting. Occasionally car chases would be successful if the rum-runner abandoned his car and took off on foot. Then both he and the moonshine could be confiscated. But more often than not,

____

[64] Miller, "The Revenue," 199.

[65] Alexander, *The Corn-Liquor Chase*, 20.

deputies simply ran them out of the county, turning the chase over to the next county's jurisdiction. Roy acknowledged the futility of attempting to catch rum-runners. The rum-runner was rarely followed into the new jurisdiction unless suspected of more than simply transporting moonshine. He remarked it was only a misdemeanor, the runner would be out on the road the next night, and more often than not the deputy could not chase down the runner's automobile. The majority of the deputies' times were spent on crimes other than misdemeanors, and not focused on people the majority of Appalachian society didn't believe were dangerous criminals to begin with.[66]

Roy's attitude toward moonshine is apparent in his several statements regarding the industry and its participants. He stated, "Ninety-nine per cent of the men who drove liquor cars were law-abiding citizens in all other ways. They didn't see hauling corn liquor as criminal. It was their work and their excitement -- an extension of prohibition rum-running that still had great public acceptance."[67] In just one remark Roy turns the attention to vital debatable components of moonshining. Many southerners did not consider moonshiners criminals. Supported by the sentiment behind the Whiskey Rebellion, the right to grow crops, belief in independence, and capitalism, the southern farmer did not consider producing a more profitable product from his crop as criminal. Growing the crop, carrying

---

[66] Alexander, *The Corn-Liquor Chase*, 13, 21-24.

[67] Alexander, *The Corn-Liquor Chase*, 13.

the supplies to hidden stills, making the mash and producing the whiskey, protecting the stills from revenuers, and then selling to the middle man, who stood to benefit the most financially, was all very hard work.[68]

General public acceptance was also a factor in the ability to control bootlegging. According to Roy, rum-runners who were caught were generally charged with transporting and often reckless driving. He remarked only a few would serve any time. Most paid a fine or would turn witness against another producer in order to reduce any fine or sentence. The runner was a businessman, often with backing. As evidence that people often looked the other way, Roy observed that those who sold premium liquor to judges would post a bond and be back out on the road the next night. Still operators usually served more time than the rum-runners, since making and selling a product without paying taxes was against the law. Roy observed during the Hoover presidency the average moonshiner was doing better than many others. He also claimed the public often looked up at the farmer, who was a hard worker and not sitting around waiting for a handout. Roy himself remarked, "I respected a lot of liquor-makers."[69] He also infers in his interview that his love of automobiles and the excitement of chasing cars was more the draw than the morality of halting the activity. He admired the rum-runners'

---

[68] Alexander, *The Corn-Liquor Chase*, 14.

[69] Alexander, *The Corn-Liquor Chase*, 14.

courage and driving ability, and if they weren't able catch the runner, Roy insisted "he hadn't [really] done anything wrong [anyway]."[70]

Roy Alexander's beliefs about moonshiners were not anomalies. Ruby Watts in *Our Appalachia* states in his oral history interview, "When the people got in trouble on making moonshine and selling and either myself or some of my deputies caught anybody, I would always go with them to court and try my best to get them out if they promised to quit, and I had right good success out of it. I always thought it was better if we could get them to promise to quit [and] get them on probation than it was to prosecute them and send them to jail for four to six months; then they'd go right back into it."[71] Cora Frazier, also interviewed in *Our Appalachia,* was a schoolteacher in Colson, Kentucky in the early 1940s. She talks of finding a still in the woods behind the school, and she knew some of the boys were going to the still during breaks. She called a conference before school and said to the students, "Now, boys and girls, the families that are connected with anything up here in the willow bed, you tell your daddies that I said to get it away from my school and I'll never go to any officers or anybody. All I want is that away from the school and they'll never be another word said on my part."[72] She goes

---

[70] Alexander, *The Corn-Liquor Chase*, 3, 24.

[71] Shackelford, *Our Appalachia*, 36.

[72] Shackelford, *Our Appalachia*, 56.

on to remark in her interview that she knew how desperate they all were in trying to make a living, and while she was against making moonshine she didn't want any trouble.[73]

Charlie Rice is quoted in "The Appalachian Image Reexamined," "I used to make moonshine whiskey when I couldn't get a job, and I made good moonshine whiskey when I couldn't pass the [medical] examination to work in the mines. And I made good moonshine whiskey and sold to them boys by the book and they bootlegged it out. And they were just as honest as the day is long."[74] Another interview of Hester Mullins in *Our Appalachia* talks of not appreciating her heritage until she was older and began working on oral history projects. She feels the majority of her generation grew up as selfish brats, focused only on their needs. When her grandmother told stories of how hard it was to live through the Depression and one had to do what was necessary to survive, she discussed how moonshining was a necessity for many people. Hester remarked to her grandmother that she would have starved before she did that and she was ashamed of her grandfather for making moonshine. In later years, in talking to her grandmother, Hester realized that her grandfather was an honorable, hard-working man who had served in positions such as magistrate, school teacher, storekeeper, tool handyman, and

---

[73] Shackelford, *Our Appalachia*, 56.

[74] Birdwhistell and Allen, "The Appalachian Image Reexamined," 297.

barn builder. Hester realized he did whatever was necessary to support his family, and had she been in his boots she would have done the same.[75]

Hester Mullins was ashamed that she had been ashamed of her grandfather. When she began to understand the history, she became proud of her heritage and understood how hard people had fought to survive. She likened her naivety and misunderstanding to those outside Appalachian culture who are quick to judge and misinterpret or stereotype the people.[76] These oral histories are integral clues into the lives of Appalachia and they help push back on the stereotype. By giving voice to the hard-working, spirited and determined people of Appalachia, hopefully many of the accounts from the past from both historians and media will be overridden.

Conclusion

Appalachia is a region ripe for analysis with new cultural history methods. New cultural history illustrates the progression from the scientific analysis of data and events to a cultural perspective, in which people create their historical interpretations of their world. Most importantly, this methodology builds on former vital methods and traditions while adding its new methods and views; all of which broadens

---

[75] Shackelford, *Our Appalachia*, 10
[76] Shackelford, *Our Appalachia*, 10

the ever-growing historical fabric. The opinions on and studies of Appalachia are as diverse as the cultures and persons inhabiting the region. The overarching theme in these studies is the dispute over whether Appalachian people made their culture, or if the culture made the people. Assisted by new cultural history, genealogical research and an infusion of oral histories reveal voluminous evidence of the region's history and illustrate a land created by people with pride in their long, hard-fought American heritage.

In response to what some feel the many Appalachian studies and material have produced, that is, poor at best and stymieing at worst in its characterizations and results, there has been an emergence of numerous other historians and authors from newer historiographical schools of thoughts. Williams, Shackelford, Billings, Birdwhistell, and Allen, to name a few, have felt compelled to produce material and perform research to help dispel these myths and promote Appalachian culture in what they view its trueness and accuracy. For some, Appalachia connotes a land of rugged pastoralism, with patriotic individualistic settlers and the birthplace of countless modern day American societal aspects such as its music (including country, bluegrass, and blues), NASCAR, literary achievements, and mountain craftwork. For others, it connotes the land of *Deliverance* and hillbillies. New material, in response to previous studies, has strengthened the cultural interpretation aspect in the debate between scholars of what they perceive Appalachia's deserved reputation to be. This newer material has enabled Appalachia to fight back against the stereotype and reveals a group of rich people – rich in their beliefs, traditions, and ways of life. Oral histories from the region not only supplement Appalachia's long and magnificent history, but also support that many of her settlers created their culture with pride, tradition, and free will; people "whose lives quietly shaped the region." [77]

---

[77] Shackelford, *Our Appalachia*, 5.

Bibliography

Alexander, Joseph. "The Forties." In The Alexanders: Memoirs of a North Carolinian Family, 1-5. Rocklin: Alexact Genealogy, 2009.

___________, "The Music." In The Alexanders: Memoirs of a North Carolinian Family. Rocklin, CA: Alexact Genealogy, 2009.

Alexander, Roy. Power Speech: The Quickest Route to Business and Personal Success. New York: AMACOM, Division of American Management Association, 1986.

Alexander, Ruth Upshaw. Memoirs in Chalkdust: My 31 Years as an Appalachian Schoolteacher. Fairview, NC: Oral History interview by Roy Alexander and personal memoir, transcript, private collection, 1997-1998.

Alexander, William Roy. The Corn-Liquor Chase: Memoirs of a 1930s Appalachian Deputy Sheriff. Fairview, NC: Oral history interview by Roy Alexander, private collection, 1985.

Algeo, Katie. "Locals on Local Color: Imagining Identity in Appalachia." Southern Cultures 9, no. 4 (Winter 2003): 27-54.

Anderson, Margaret. "Education in Appalachia: Past Failures and Future Prospects." Journal of Marriage and Family 26, no. 4 (November 1964): 443-446.

Appalachian Regional Commission. http://www.arc.gov/index.jsp (accessed December 7, 2009).

Biggers, Jeff. The United States of Appalachia: How Southern Mountaineers Brought Independence, Culture, and Enlightenment to America. Emeryville, CA: Shoemaker & Hoard, 2006.

Billings, Dwight B., and Kathleen M. Blee. The Road to Poverty: The Making of Wealth and Hardship in Appalachia. Cambridge: Cambridge University Press, 2000.

Billings, Dwight. "Culture and Poverty in Appalachia: A Theoretical Discussion and Empirical Analysis." Social

Forces (University of North Carolina Press) 53, no. 2 (December 1974): 315-323.

Birdwhistell, Terry L, and Susan Emily Allen. "The Appalachian Image Reexamined: An Oral History View of Eastern Kentucky." The Register of the Kentucky Historical Society 81, no. 3 (1983): 287-302.

Brown, Tom. "Sugar in the Gourd: Preserving Applachian Traditions." Music Educators Journal 70, no. 3 (November 1983): 52-55.

Campbell, John Charles. The Southern Highlander and His Homeland. New York: The Russell Sage Foundation, 1921.

Candler, Allen D. Colonel William Candler of Georgia: His Ancestry and Progeny. Atlanta: The Franklin Printing & Publishing Company, 1902.

Dietrich, Julia C. "The Gaelic Roots of A-Prefixing in Appalachian English." American Speech (Duke University Press) 56, no. 4 (Winter 1981): 314.

Erikson, Kai T. Everything in its Path: Destruction of Community in the Buffalo Creek Flood. New York: Simon & Schuster, 1978.

Harkins, Anthony. Hillbilly: A Cultural History of an American Icon. New York, NY: Oxford University Press, 2005.

Howell, Martha, and Walter Prevenier. From Reliable Sources: An Introduction to Historical Methods. Ithaca: Cornell University Press, 2001.

Langrall, Peggy. "Appalachian Folk Music: From Foothills to Footlights." Music Educators Journal (MENC: The National Association for Music Education) 72, no. 7 (March 1986): 37-39.

Luebke, B.H., and John Fraser Hart. "Migration from a Southern Appalachian Community." Land Economics (University of Wisconsin Press) 34, no. 1 (February 1958): 44-53.

MacDonald, Donnie. "Scottish Gaelic, lecture notes taken by author." 2002.

Malone, Bill C., and David Stricklin. Southern
        Music/American Music. University of Kentucky Press,
        2003.
McCormick, Mack. "The Musical Resources of American
        Folklife." Music Educators Journal 56, no. 1
        (September 1969): 47-50.
McNeil, W.K. Appalachian Images in Folk and Popular
        Culture. Edited by W.K. McNeil. Original from Indiana
        University: UMI Research Press, 1989.
Miller, Wilbur R. "The Revenue: Federal Law Enforcement in
        the Mountain South, 1870-1900." The Journal of
        Southern History 55, no. 2 (May 1989): 195-216.
Ostendorf, Ann. "Song Catchers, Ballad Makers, and New
        Social Historians: The Historiography of Appalachian
        Music." Tennessee Historical Quarterly 63 (Fall 2004):
        193-202.
Rehder, John B. Appalachian Folkways. Baltimore: The John
        Hopkins University Press, 2004.
Shackelford, Laurel. Our Appalachia: An Oral History. Edited
        by Bill Weinberg and Laurel Shackelford. University
        Press of Kentucky, reprint, 1988.
Smith, Martha. "Appalachian Music is Alive and Kicking."
        Appalachia 6, no. 1 (September 1972): 26-33.
Sondley, Foster Alexander. Asheville and Buncombe County.
        Asheville: The Citizen Company, 1922.
Williams, John Alexander. Appalachia: A History. The
        University of North Carolina Press, 2001.

The Music

Joseph Alexander

There was always music. My earliest memories include music in some form. We listened to scratchy music on our big Philco radio. We sang, we whistled, we hummed, and we played combs and spoons. It might have not been good music, but if we noticed any deficiencies, it didn't reduce our need for it. We had family music sessions with Buh playing her Gibson Junior mandolin and Pappy strumming his Kay guitar, and the rest of us trying to sing whatever was played. We had some very non-current songbooks and they were the basis and extent of our repertoire. Buh read music and played from the books while Pappy, playing by ear, backed her up. This arrangement inherently limited the songs we could play and sing as Pappy only played in the keys of D and G and sometimes C. We performed all the D, G, and C songs in our songbooks and ignored the others as being undesirable. Pappy called any song outside of those three keys as being played in "E flat R". If we suggested an unacceptable song, Pappy would fuss and call our request "an old E flat R song." If someone requested that he play a song heard on the radio, he would characterize the song as being impossible to play because it was in the key of E flat R. When I became old enough to try to learn to play the guitar and mandolin, I lived in dread of running into an E flat R song because I knew that I would never be able to play such a difficult piece. So I dutifully learned D, G and C positions and ignored the other keys while trying to control my E flat R phobia. Years later I learned there was, indeed, an "E flat" key, but I never identified the key of "R", and the key of "E flat R" has never been explained in any of the music books that I have read.

Our household music capability received a serious upgrade while we were living in Newport News. My brother, Roy, was working at a butcher shop after school, on Saturdays, and during the summer. (As far as I can determine from Roy's accounts of this job, his primary responsibility at the shop was to mix ketchup into the expired ground meat to make it look fresher. It was also during this time that Roy decided to never again eat chicken, but never explained to me how he came to this very un-southern decision). Having become economically solvent, one of Roy's first purchases was a wind-up phonograph, and we now had the ability to play records any time we felt the need to listen to a song. The tonal fidelity of the wind-up phonograph roughly approximated, but did not exceed, that of the Philco radio. Roy bought only Roy Acuff and Gene Autry records, and that was perfectly acceptable to us. We were fascinated with this marvelous machine, and we played all of Roy's records over and over and over. The phonograph would play both sides of the 78 record on one wind-up, and we were directed by the Victrola's instructions to change the needle after each record was played. Due to the expense and inconvenience involved, we only changed the needle when the mood struck us, which was not all that often. The consequence of our needle procedure modification was a steady deterioration in the tonal fidelity of Mr. Autry and Mr. Acuff until a level of bare recognition was reached, but we still continued to play them over and over and over. Roy Acuff told us of the wreck on the highway when he "didn't hear nobody pray" and Gene Autry sang about spurs that jingle, jangle, jingle.

Pappy talked a lot about mountain music while we lived in Virginia. He called it "old-time music" or "old-timey music." He would tell us that old-time music could only be heard (and played, evidently) in the mountains of North Carolina. He said that some people tried to play his music at the Grand Old Opry, but they played it wrong. He further said that his music could never be written or recorded. (As it was discovered later, there were records of Pappy's music at that time, but none by Autry or Acuff). With our move back to the mountains, Pappy began a search for old-time musicians. There were no phones in our community, nor folks who had the funds to pay for phone service had it been offered, so Pappy would make impromptu visits to the homes of those he thought might have an interest and/or permission to play music at our home on Saturday night. Pappy's first recruits didn't work out so well, and it began to appear doubtful that we were ever going to hear the music that had been described for years in terms that evoked such mystery and anticipation. Then through a chance conversation with our mail carrier, Pappy learned that, not only was the mailman a mandolin player, he also knew other pickers. The mailman's name was Red Dills and he knew of a five-string banjo player, Homer Israel, who lived in Fletcher.   Pappy set out on a mission to find Homer and learned that Homer knew a fiddler, Johnny Miller. When located, Johnny agreed to join the others at our house on Saturday night, and with the addition of Pappy's rhythm guitar, we had a band of old-time musicians. And they were good, but their personal lives were not without complications.

Homer, Red, and Johnny had been playing for square dances and other events in the community for some time, and had not impressed their wives in a positive way with their behavior while out of the sphere of spousal supervision. On one occasion, Homer returned home on the early morning side of a music night out in a very unsteady condition. When his tardiness and lack of equilibrium was pointed out to him, he did what any good banjo player would have done - he knocked a hole in the wall with his fist. It was a substantial wall and Homer broke several bones in his hand. Homer wasn't allowed to play any old-time music for a while but because of his broken hand he was unable to play during his penalty time anyhow. When he finally was allowed to come to our house again, he showed up with his now refurbished banjo that he had reworked during his quiet time. He also was out-and-about under a new set of strict rules that dictated how long he could play and where he could not go after leaving our house. One of the improvements he had made to his Gibson banjo during his down time was a replacement of the frets. He had chosen aluminum frets instead of the conventional brass frets because they had been endorsed by his idol, Earl Scruggs, and he was excited about the improvement. Unfortunately, pronunciation of the word "aluminum" did not come easy to Homer and it came out, "alum num yum". We enjoyed hearing his description of his new frets and always asked him to tell us about them.

Johnny, on the other hand, had an even more spotty record of returning home at the expected time - if at all. Sometimes during a night out, Johnny would lose track of where his home might be located and would not return home until his memory recovered, and that might take some time. Johnny spent some nights at taxpayer expense in the county lockup until his homing instincts were restored to a minimum level, and unhappily for Johnny, a return home after these memory failures meant a suffering of the consequences awaiting him there. Red was our stabilizing soul. He came into the house, played excellent mandolin until time to leave and then went home (as far as I know). During the night, he might utter four or five sentences and then only after extreme encouragement.

Homer, Johnny and Red would always arrive for the Saturday night music at the same time. I never did know how they did that, but my guess would be a central rendezvous followed by a three-car convoy to our house, this so none of them would have to come in the house alone.   The players would take seats in our living room, place their instrument cases on the floor beside their chair and then pretend that the instruments did not exist. Small talk would be exchanged until Pappy would say, "Homer, how 'bout getting' that banjer outa the case and let me see it." Homer would produce the banjo and there would be discussion about his latest improvements to it and how he was still dissatisfied with its sound. This ritual would be repeated with the other players until all instruments were out of their cases and the tuning session would begin. The time spent on tuning the four instruments varied, but was never quick. There was no standard tuning as no tuning instruments such as a pitch pipe or tuning fork were used as a reference. Instead, all the other instruments would be tuned to the one that seemed to be the closest to some non-standard tuning at the outset.   The instruments were almost always tuned well above standard because string changes were not common, and all of us would tune higher to compensate for the lack of life in the old strings. The strings would ultimately reach their upper tensile limit and begin to break, and that would tell us it was time to lower the tuning to some other non-standard level. At the end of the tuning session, it was not at all uncommon for the player who provided the first tuning reference to have to re-tune to the now higher level of non-standard tuning. But, now they were ready to play, and everyone was careful not to break the ancient old-time musician's code of simply beginning to play a song without going through the pre-song ritual they all knew and endorsed. Before the first bar of music was heard, each player would offer his instrument to every other musician saying, "Here take this thing - I can't play it." After refusals all around, Pappy would say, "Johnny, let's hear a little of that Cripple Creek." Johnny would protest that he had not played Cripple Creek in years and didn't even remember the tune. He would then proceed to fiddle Cripple Creek to perfection and with an ease that would suggest that the years away from Cripple Creek might have ended in a practice session just before leaving for our house that night. Now that the first-song-of-the-night code had been breached, the group would begin a journey through their repertoire of songs and the music would improve with the progression of the night. They played "the two Sallies"; Sally Goodin and Sally Ann, they played Cumberland Gap, Black Mountain Rag, Asheville (a localized version of Bucking Mule), Sourwood Mountain, Soldier's Joy, and many more they had learned from their kin who had learned it from their kin, ad infinitum.

Pappy recognized the challenges that faced him in managing his band. He knew that if he did not provide some intoxicants, he might lose Johnny and Homer. He also knew that too much Old Crow or white lightening would denigrate the quality of the fiddle and banjo, and also might incite more penalty periods. His whiskey rationing procedures were effective and also became very predictable to those of us who witnessed the ritual more than once. It went like this. When the group took their first break to smoke and relax, Pappy would say to Homer and Johnny, "You boys come on out to the kitchen - I have something to show you." There were no mixers or ice cubes or any other condiments usually consumed with alcoholic beverages - just straight whiskey sipped out of the bottle/jug. About five minutes later, the three would return and a noticeable improvement in congeniality would be obvious. This ritual would be repeated at Pappy-determined intervals throughout the night and the band would play on 'til the early morning hours.

Word of the band got around the community, and other musicians would appear at our Saturday night music parties. I don't know if someone invited them or if they just came. Though I never met the wives of the original pickers, the new occasional musicians would sometimes appear with their wives. My initial appraisal of the wives' motivation for attending the party was incorrect as it soon became obvious that they had not come to listen to the music. They came to oversee their husband's return home while limiting his ingestion of consumables before that time was determined.

These ladies appeared without introduction, explanation or acknowledgment, and they sat silently and observed throughout the evening. The ladies had no names as far as we knew until Bruce came home for a visit. Bruce thought the ladies should have names. He named them all "Myrtle".

One of these come-lately musicians caused the only real dust-up among the members of our original group that I can remember or knew of during those years. Someone who had not played with us before brought an electric, amplified guitar to our house one Saturday night. To the old-time pickers, an amplified instrument was an insult to their music and they were incensed by the intrusion. The transgressing guitar player plugged in his guitar and proceeded to rattle the windows and the nerves of the old-time musicians. The fiddle, banjo, mandolin and acoustic guitar could not be heard above the distorted din of the Sears and Roebuck guitar and amplifier. Without a word, Homer, Johnny and Red packed up their instruments and departed. They did not come back until Pappy finally and firmly convinced them that there would never again be any amplified instruments allowed in the house. And, as far as I know, Pappy kept his word.

Occasionally, the band would be invited to play for a private party in someone's home. There was no fee involved for their performance, and I don't believe they would have accepted money had it been offered. Payment would have created an obligation and that would have compromised their independence, which would have been unacceptable. Pappy was very impressed by the extravagance of one of these parties. At breakfast the morning after the party, he told us that the folks giving the party spared no expense. "Why, beer and pretzels were served," he said.

The groups' insistence on autonomy and independence became even more evident when Roy and his longtime friend, Pat Phillips came to visit. Pat was writing for Good Housekeeping magazine and was planning an article on the music and musicians in our group. Pappy made the rounds to get the players together, and he told them there would be a photographer and someone present that might ask them some questions about their music. All agreed to be there - none came. That left Pat with a photographer and no story subjects or material. Good marketing people, though, don't let small setbacks stop a story, so pictures were taken of me playing the fiddle and Pat wrote the story based on what we told her about the group. I did not receive a single performance contract offer from this article's appearance.

As time went on, it became more difficult for Pappy to get his group together, but while they were still playing occasionally, an Asheville radio station, WSKY, invited them to play on the station's country music show. The date was set and all agreed to meet at the radio station - and they did. Through a timing glitch or other bad luck, they arrived at the station a couple of hours before the show. They were put into a room where they could tune their instruments, but after tuning they had time on their hands. Johnny announced that he had to go meet somebody and would be back in time for the show. This did not bode well for the group's engagement, but no one commented on Johnny's departure. True to his word, Johnny returned with time to spare, though his demeanor seemed to have changed somewhat, and it was time for the final tuning before going on the air. Everyone picked up their instruments. Johnny tightened and rosined up his bow and carefully lifted the fiddle to his shoulder. He lowered his chin to the instrument and adjusted his body position. Then he closed his eyes as he brought the bow up to the fiddle's strings and with one energetic and enthusiastic stroke, fired the bow across the room like a javelin. Johnny's sidemen looked at the bow now in repose on the other side of the WSKY room, exchanged looks of resignation, packed up their instruments and left the station.

The WSKY non-engagement signaled the end of Pappy's old-time group. They had played together for an impressive number of years and had survived more than one adventure along the way. They played hundreds of songs; hundreds of time, and the music was just as enjoyable the last time as the first. They played the songs that Pappy had talked about so many times while we were living away from the only acceptable old-time music area - the mountains of North Carolina. Fiddle dance tunes made up the majority of the music, and though some of the songs had words, they were not sung. Singing was not a part of the mountain music. The fiddle songs had a definite Irish flavor and it was not hard to accept the belief that they had been played by previous generations of musicians eerily similar to our players. With just a gentle nudge of the imagination, one might be able to visualize a long ago Saturday night gathering of prior generation folk in the Old Country, fiddling and dancing to Sally Anne while tasting a bit of the Irish Whiskey. There might have been whispers among those present about a participant's home that was said to have an unexplained and undiscussed hole in the wall. The fiddler just might have suffered a punishment period for a recent late and impaired return to his home. The fiddler's wife just might have been named Myrtle.

I wonder where we picked up these traits that are so difficult to explain.

North Carolinian Youth on the Home Front in World War II

Diane Alexander

The South, and particularly the Appalachian region, has long been stigmatized with backwardness and poverty. The post-World War II South suffered a loss of industry and population, realizing the largest outmigration of Americans to date, as Appalachian and southern regions were decimated by the shift of populations to urban areas. In a later era, the War on Poverty in the 1960s would bring desperate poverty in a "strange" region with "strange" people to mainstream Americans' televisions. Nonetheless, at least for a time, the South, and notably North Carolina, was on equal footing throughout the Great Depression and World War II. For several decades in the twentieth century, North Carolina was no less poverty-stricken than other regions of the United States; no less patriotic than other Americans during wartime were; and no less affected by devastating losses and hardship through the Depression and World War II. The Depression and wartime-America leveled the playing field for all citizens. Indeed, North Carolina represented as well as any other states, even surpassing, national contributions in several areas.

Although resistant at first to fight another war after the traumas of World War I, North Carolinians were not alone in isolationist thoughts with their fellow Americans. After the bombing of Pearl Harbor, however, North Carolina, as did other states, leapt into action with the U.S. entry into World War II. Governor J. Melville Broughton declared in a speech "not since the beginning of our national history has our democracy been so threatened."[1] North Carolinians solemnly heeded instructions by their governor and President Roosevelt in his "fireside chats" and the state mobilized quickly. John Duvall asserts, "North Carolina contributed enormous resources and energy to the Allied victory in World War II."[2] North Carolinian youth were a large factor in these efforts.

For those who came of age during World War II, their experiences and remembrances greatly differed. Some remembered a united time, full of adventure and new things, while others saw their families dislocated or devastated by fathers, brothers, and uncles who never returned home from the war. All recall vastly differing experiences across a wide spectrum and every remembrance was unique. Regardless of their experiences, the youth of America answered the call issued to all citizens and they proved themselves patriotic, obedient, and hardworking. North Carolinian youths took their

---

[1] John S. Duvall, "North Carolina's Wartime Miracle: Defending the Nation," *Learn NC* (2008), http://www.learnnc.org/lp/editions/nchist-sampler/5907 (accessed December 27, 2014).

[2] Duvall, *Wartime Miracle.*

roles in the war efforts seriously and as confirmation of this, made notable and substantial contributions to the World War II American home front.

The largest contributions that youth made to the war movement were with scrap metal drives and victory gardens. Through his "fireside chats," Roosevelt, encouraged--even demanded-- that Americans do all they could to win the war. They must make sacrifices, endure hardship, accept rationing, and invest in war bonds. He reminded Americans that these sacrifices were nothing compared to what Europeans under Hitler's regime were enduring. He went on to state that sacrifice was not the proper term as, "When, at the end of this great struggle we shall have saved our free way of life, we shall have made no 'sacrifice.'"[3] This filtered through Americans, all the way to the youngest family members.

Wartime posters and propaganda were widely utilized and populous, conjecturing unpatriotic accusations if one did not do everything possible to aid the war effort. Carolina Power & Light Company in Asheville, North Carolina was one of innumerable propagandists that encouraged metal collections, urging people to save and collect every scrap of metal they could, which would in turn be used in the war effort

---

[3] "The War at Home: Calling for Sacrifice: Excerpt from Radio Address by President Franklin Roosevelt, April 28, 1942," *Learn NC* (2015), http://www.learnnc.org/lp/editions/nchist-worldwar/5845 (accessed January 28, 2015).

for materiel. They encouraged youth to mobilize, proclaiming in one of their ads, "There's a job for girls in this war, too!" In addition to coordinating with their Girl Scout troops to collect scrap material, the company suggested girls help their mothers with the housework so that mothers would have more time to devote to local war activities, such as the Red Cross. Barbara Lashley remembers her Girl Scout troop going door to door collecting scrap metal, collecting everything from car parts to pots and pans. In addition to collecting the scrap materials, she also went to St. Joseph's Hospital every Saturday morning and rolled bandages for Bundles for Britain. Joan Quinn recalls collecting aluminum foil as the most fun activity. "Kids would collect foil, often from gum wrappers and cigarette packs, and make them into balls of foil. Kids would compete to see who could make the biggest ball of foil on the block."[4]

North Carolinians, eager to do their part throughout the war, stepped up to the challenge issued by President Roosevelt to ration, produce their own food, and feed soldiers. Programs such as scrap metal drives and planting victory gardens were methods by which every American could participate. North Carolina's 4-H clubs were crucial to the efforts of food campaigns throughout the war. Popular wartime food

---

[4] Reid Chapman and Deborah Miles, *Images of America: Asheville and Western North Carolina in World War II* (Charleston, SC: Arcadia Publishing, 2006), 37; Richard Panchyk, *World War II for Kids: A History* (Chicago: Chicago Review Press, 2002), 62.

programs included the Food for Freedom, Victory Garden, and Food for Fighters programs. Victory gardens were a method to mobilize all, including the youth, to make a substantial contribution to the war effort. The principle of the gardens had developed during the Depression when the government had encouraged gardening and canning as a way for people to feed themselves. Victory gardens were a stepped-up version of self-sufficiency. The more food people supplied, the more could be sent to the troops, and the less rationing and scarcity of food in the nation. More precisely, the more people grew themselves, the more that commercial agriculture could grow for the military. Although the majority of Americans lived in rural areas, victory gardens sprang up "in strange nooks and crannies all over U.S." They were even grown on rooftops and balconies. Eighteen million gardens alone were planted in 1943.[5]

According to David Walbert, "In 1943, 20 million victory gardens produced more than 40 percent of the fresh vegetables grown that year in the United States."[6] To demonstrate the contributions these food campaigns made, the winner of the "Feed a Fighter" campaign in North Carolina

---

[5] David Walbert, "Victory Gardens," *Learn NC* (2015) http://www.learnnc.org/lp/editions/nchist-sampler/5883 (accessed January 28, 2015); Duvall, *Wartime Miracle.*

[6] David Walbert, "Enlistment for Victory (1943)," *Learn NC* (2015) http://www.learnnc.org/lp/editions/nchist-worldwar/6050 (accessed January 28, 2015).

raised enough food alone to feed 34 service members for a year. Sullivan Fisher and Ena Vann Lewis were the state winners in the program and each won a $100 war bond. Because of wartime projects and campaigns, 4-H club membership in North Carolina increased to 93,000 members, more than doubling the membership a decade earlier. With each of these members urged to do their best for the war effort, the contributions made by North Carolinian youths were considerable. Youth campaigns through the 4-H clubs in North Carolina were so prolific in their campaigns they won the honor of naming two of the ships in the U.S. fleet, the USS *Tyrell* and the USS *Cassius Hudson*.[7]

According to Roy Thomas, North Carolina teachers of agriculture "answered the challenge of the war effort." These teachers were the lead coordinators in various agricultural projects. Even with the loss of 125 teachers to the armed forces, Thomas demonstrates significant achievement in these programs, indicating among some of the accomplishments over 10,000 acres increased over 1941 in victory gardens, over 600,000 poultry heads increased, over 42,000 head of swine,

---

[7] Walbert, "Victory Gardens;" Walbert, "Enlistment for Victory;" Amy Manor, "4-H and Home Demonstration during World War II," *NCSU Libraries: Green 'N' Growing - The History of Home Demonstration and 4-H Youth Development in North Carolina* (September 19, 2006), http://www.lib.ncsu.edu/specialcollections/greenngrowing/essay_wwii.html (accessed January 26, 2015).

and almost 9,300 heads of cattle increased. He additionally states that North Carolinians collected more than 6,000,000 pounds of scrap metal. The contribution of North Carolina's youth was significant and sizeable.[8]

Less enjoyable than war effort activities and campaigns but just as necessary, American youths learned also to do their part in air raid drills and blackouts. Despite World War II being largely fought on foreign soil, the war came to the United States, both in the bombing of Pearl Harbor and in German U-boat activity targeting U.S. ships in the Atlantic Ocean. For those in the eastern coastal regions during World War II, many remember the war as practically in their backyard. Because of the increased oceanic activity, air raid drills--with accompanying blackouts--were serious business, particularly in the Virginia and North Carolina coastal areas. The threat of bombing, actualized by both the London Blitz and the attack on Pearl Harbor, was a legitimate concern. During air raid drills, a siren would sound, signaling a drill. Everyone would have to cover their windows, turn off all lights, and remain inside. Authorities would patrol the areas to ensure everyone was compliant.

Margaret Rogers, a Wilmington, North Carolina, resident, remembers her mother's daily routine of pinning

---

[8] Roy H. Thomas, "High-School Vocational Teachers and the War Effort in Agriculture," *The High School Journal* (University of North Carolina Press) 26, no. 1/2 (Jan-Feb 1943): 16.

quilts over the windows. One window had metal venetian blinds rather than quilts. During a blackout, Margaret crept to the window to look outside, stating the metal venetian blinds made their typical clinking sound. Within seconds, a soldier furiously knocked on their door. Margaret's mother answered the door and the soldier asked if she wanted that child, stating that she had almost been shot. Her mother responded with a promise that her daughter would never do that again and Margaret confirms she did not, stating that even in a blackout her mother could find her bottom! Joe Alexander, a Fairview, North Carolina, resident, was six years old when his family temporarily moved to Newport News, Virginia when his father took a position as a burner at the shipyard. He remembers the drills in the Hampton Roads area, stating, "The war became worse and I was scared at times. We had blackouts during recurring air raid drills, and when we inadvertently left a bathroom light on one night during a drill, we received a fine by the local wartime authority."[9]

Lionel Gilgo was a resident of Portsmouth Island, near Cape Hatteras. A particularly active area of U-boat activity, his area was known as "Torpedo Junction." Gilgo recalls the houses shaking and windows rattling, after which residents would go outside to "look for the red glow from yet another

---

[9] *UNC TV: Home - The Acts - Full of Promise*, (2015) http://wwii.unctv.org/the-acts/full-of-promise (accessed December 28, 2014); Alexander, *The Forties*.

ship being hit." He recalls the fear that Germans would come ashore. "Everywhere you went, every home you went into, there was talk of 'wonder how many ships will be sunk tonight and how many explosions we'll hear.'"[10] Charles Stowe and his father had an extremely close call in Hatteras. Their fishing boat nearly struck a U-boat rising to the surface. His father thought it was another fishing vessel and told Charles to keep going, but Charles said, "Dad, that is a German submarine!" They turned around and got out just in time.[11]

Despite the terrifying blackouts and fears of Germans, children remained ever courageous and patriotic throughout the war. Even the youngest child wanted to contribute. Mrs. Julia Ray of Asheville, North Carolina, recalls her five-year-old daughter accompanying her frequently to the local courthouse to pass out donuts and coffee to the departing troops to make them feel they were not on their own when they left. Her daughter repeatedly begged to help, so they dressed her in a custom-made military uniform and gave her a basket filled with donuts. She would go with them every time at six a.m. to pass out food to the soldiers.[12]

---

[10] *UNC TV: Home - The Acts – War on the Home Front*, (2015) http://wwii.unctv.org/the-acts/full-of-promise (accessed December 28, 2014).

[11] Kevin P. Duffus, "When World War II Was Fought off North Carolina's Beaches," *Learn NC* (Spring 2008), www.learnnc.org (accessed January 24, 2015), 1.

[12] Chapman and Miles, *Images of America, 38.*

Children everywhere wanted to do what they could. Joe Alexander recalls him and his friend, Mike Spangler deciding they should go to Germany to "help our boys fight." They collected "weapons, some fearful sticks and menacing stones, put them in a washtub with a pull-string attached" and told Joe's mother they were going off to fight the war. He says she gave her blessing and they "departed for the front." They knew that Germany was across the ocean, so they logically set off for the nearest body of water, which was the Chesapeake Bay, about ten blocks away from their home. After reaching the Bay, they discovered a chain link fence preventing any further advance and as they were preparing their strategy to breach the barrier, Mike's parents drove up and returned the boys home. Joe recalls receiving a severe lecture about crossing streets. The rule was the boys could go anywhere in the neighborhood as long as they did not cross any streets. Joe feigns indignation remembering the scolding, justifying that, after all, they had told his mother they were bound for Germany and that it should have been clear in order to fulfill that mission that crossing streets would be a necessity.[13]

Despite somber and serious attention paid to home front activities, such as air raid drills and blackouts, curiosity and mischief of children remains eternal. Parents learned to strike a balance between rearing patriotic, obedient children, who

---

[13] Alexander, *The Forties*.

represented their nation well and helped the war effort, and allowing their children to "mobilize for the war" in their age-appropriate methods. Children learned balance as well, learning how to distinguish between acting patriotically and dangerously, and they found many of their transgressions with patriotic good intentions forgiven. The patriotic fervor of North Carolina in World War II resounded heavily in the youth.

World War II launched what would become one of the largest migrations in U.S. history – the outmigration of Appalachians into U.S. urban areas, beginning with migration during the war for war industry jobs and continuing for decades after the war. This outmigration radically shifted North Carolina's demographics. Wartime migration took place for various reasons. Some voluntarily moved to war jobs - some temporarily and some permanently - and others were forcefully relocated. North Carolina became a flourishing region during the war, particularly with the building of several military bases. According to Ronald Eller, North Carolina had more soldiers than any other state by the end of 1942 and "became one of the leading states contributing to the nation's growing military efforts."[14] Some families were unfortunate to live in areas where the land they lived on was needed for war efforts. Marlene Blake recalls receiving an eviction notice for

____

[14] Ronald D. Eller, *Uneven Ground: Appalachia since 1945* (Lexington: University Press of Kentucky, 2009), 13; Duvall, *Wartime Miracle*.

their homestead in order to make room for Camp Lejeune. They loaded up everything they owned and all they had worked for with nowhere to go and no job prospects or idea what they were going to do. Despite this trauma, she remembers some families having it even worse. If they did not move by eviction day, soldiers loaded their belongings, drove across the boundary line, and dumped their possessions, forcefully removing them.[15]

Shortages of housing continued throughout the war for war industry workers and military personnel. Joe Alexander remembers his family taking in boarders in their two-story, two-bedroom house and participating in a process known by the Navy as "hot bedding." Shipyard workers, who worked in shifts, would sleep while others were at work and then they would rotate. This process rotated sleeping accommodations, thereby virtually increasing housing supply rather than physically. In many states and particularly coastal regions, demand for accommodations from war industry workers could not keep up with the supply.[16]

Nearly 9,000 North Carolinians died in World War II. Dan Bolden remembers the personal losses in his community. "We went to a little Methodist church down on the east side of Burlington and there was a young man who was a member there who was killed in action, and they brought his body back

---

[15] *UNC TV - Full of Promise.*
[16] Alexander, *The Forties.*

for a memorial service." Dan remembers the service member's mother's face when they gave her the flag when the service was over. He recalls "the hurt, the tears in her eyes, the loss of her only son," stating, "And that stuck with me forever, and it's still with me."[17] Numerous husbands and fathers were mourned. Many families were displaced from homes and many were part of mass migrations when war industries closed. There were celebrations as well. Loved ones returning. The end of war. And pride that they had done their part. No matter their situations and lives during the war, none would forget where they were on December 7, 1941, and none would forget their lives during World War II. Davis sums it splendidly, "The people of the state and the nation had done their part – for God and country."[18] North Carolinian youth, undeniably a crucial component of their state's war efforts, had put in a stellar performance.

---

[17] *UNC TV: Home - The Acts – Boomtown, North Carolina* (2015) http://wwii.unctv.org/the-acts/full-of-promise (accessed December 28, 2014).

[18] Anita Price Davis, *North Carolina and World War II: A Documentary Portrait* (Jefferson, NC: McFarland, 2014), 195.

Bibliography

Alexander, Joseph R., interview by Diane Alexander. The
  Forties - Oral History Interview (August 2008).

Chapman, Reid, and Deborah Miles. Images of America:
  Asheville and Western North Carolina in World War II.
  Charleston, SC: Arcadia Publishing, 2006.

Davis, Anita Price. North Carolina and World War II: A
  Documentary Portrait. Jefferson, NC: McFarland, 2014.

Duffus, Kevin P. "When World War II Was Fought off North
  Carolina's Beaches." www.learnnc.org. Spring 2008.
  www.learnnc.org (accessed January 24, 2015).

Duvall, John S. "North Carolina's Wartime Miracle: Defending
  the Nation." Learn NC. 2008.
  http://www.learnnc.org/lp/editions/nchist-sampler/5907
  (accessed December 27, 2014).

Eller, Ronald D. Uneven Ground: Appalachia since 1945.
  Lexington: University Press of Kentucky, 2009.

Manor, Amy. "4-H and Home Demonstration during World
  War II." NCSU Libraries: Green 'N' Growing - The
  History of Home Demonstration and 4-H Youth
  Development in North Carolina. September 19, 2006.
  http://www.lib.ncsu.edu/specialcollections/greenngrowi
  ng/essay_wwii.html (accessed January 26, 2015).

Panchyk, Richard. World War II for Kids: A History. Chicago:
  Chicago Review Press, 2002.

"The War at Home: Calling for Sacrifice: Excerpt from Radio
  Address by President Franklin Roosevelt, April 28,
  1942." Learn NC. 2015.
  http://www.learnnc.org/lp/editions/nchist-
  worldwar/5845 (accessed January 28, 2015).

Thomas, Roy H. "High-School Vocational Teachers and the
  War Effort in Agriculture." The High School Journal
  (University of North Carolina Press) 26, no. 1/2 (Jan-
  Feb 1943): 16-17.

UNC TV: Home - The Acts - Boomtown, North Carolina.
  2015. http://wwii.unctv.org/the-acts/boomtown-north-
  carolina (accessed December 28, 2014).

UNC TV: Home - The Acts - Full of Promise. 2015.
http://wwii.unctv.org/the-acts/full-of-promise (accessed
December 28, 2014).
UNC TV: Home - The Acts - Reflections. 2015.
http://wwii.unctv.org/the-acts/reflections (accessed
December 28, 2014).
UNC TV: Home - The Acts - War on The Home Front. 2015.
http://wwii.unctv.org/the-acts/war-on-the-home-front
(accessed December 28, 2014).
Walbert, David. "Enlistment for Victory (1943)." Learn NC.
2015. http://www.learnnc.org/lp/editions/nchist-
worldwar/6050 (accessed January 28, 2015).
—. "Victory Gardens." Learn NC. September 2009.
http://www.learnnc.org/lp/editions/nchist-sampler/5883
(accessed January 28, 2015).
—. "Winners in North Carolina's Feed a Fighter Program."
Learn NC. 2009.
http://www.learnnc.org/lp/editions/nchist-
worldwar/5887 (accessed January 28, 2015).

Pappy's Pony

Joseph Alexander

It was 1958. I had one year of State college behind me and had run out of money. I got a job as a bookkeeper at Wachovia Bank in Asheville and my plan was to save enough money to go to another year at State. My overhead was much higher than I had projected so the plan failed. Beer was $1.65 a six-pack. Gas was thirty cents a gallon. Cigarettes were twenty cents a pack. You can see why I couldn't save enough for college.

Pappy had taken on the fiddle. He was determined to become the next winner at the annual Galax, Virginia fiddling competition. Unfortunately for those living in the Fairview home, he decided that he would not spend any time with the basics, but go directly to the fun stuff - competition fiddling. He wanted to sound like the fiddle players that came to our house, Johnny Miller to be specific. To be even more specific, Johnny when he was sober. To reach his goal, he knew that he would have to have some help from someone who knew the fiddle, and Johnny was the logical fiddler to provide this help. Pappy and Johnny spent quite a few sessions together fiddling and drinking whatever Pappy had brought into the house, while Johnny would instruct Pappy on the secrets of fiddling. Johnny had an interesting method of instruction which was to play a passage at full blazing speed, then telling his student to do the same. Asking him to play the passage more slowly so one might see how he was able to produce those beautiful sounds was no help - Johnny couldn't play it slower. It was during one of these sessions that Johnny mentioned that Pappy may need an add-on device for his fiddle that would improve his playing. This is where I come into the picture.

Pappy told me he wanted me to pick up something for him at the music store in Asheville. He said he needed a "pony" for his fiddle. I tried to find out more about a fiddle pony, but Pappy was pretty vague on what it may look like, or what it may be used for, or anything more about the fiddle pony. He just said that Johnny told him he needed one for his fiddle.

The music store clerk looked blankly at me when I asked him for a fiddle pony, and I could tell that I had asked him for something he had never heard of before that day. He asked me for more information on the pony but I didn't have much more to give. I did tell him that Pappy had mentioned the pony would change the sound of the fiddle. He told me that I might be describing a mute. Now it was my turn for a blank stare during the period it took for the entire sequence of flawed communication to come to me in a rush. I told the clerk that a mute was exactly what I had come into his store to buy and left with my purchase, avoiding any further conversation concerning my original request for a pony.

The rush of revelation had been a replay in my mind of an imagined conversation between Johnny and Pappy. After some Old Crow, Johnny had told Pappy he needed a MUTE for his fiddle. After some Old Crow, Pappy heard that he needed a MULE for his fiddle. During the delay between the music session and the next time I happened to walk through on the way to my next social engagement, the MULE had morphed into a PONY.

I brought the pony home and Pappy used it religiously because Johnny told him to use it. The mute reduced the volume of the fiddle by a significant, relieving measure: and the other members of the household were very grateful for the contribution to the serenity of our home. I've always wondered what made Johnny think that Pappy needed a pony for his fiddle.

Southerners, Scots, and Settlers

Scottish Highland Games

Diane Alexander

Scottish Highland Games are an eclectic mix of entertainment that offers something for everyone. A humorous Celtic song *The Clan-Tent Cavaliers,* made popular by the Celtic group Men of Worth, is appreciated by return attendees who find the lampoon amusing as the song teases their readily-acknowledged obsessions of these games (The Clan-Tent Cavaliers, 1997). For newcomers the song neatly highlights, albeit tongue-in-cheek, the wildly diverse aspects of the games and aptly explains why these games so easily pull people back to them.

Upon entering Highland games the unique sights, smells, and sounds are like none other. There are bright kilts of every plaid color combination and design. Clan and Scottish flags, creating a vibrant spectrum, flutter in every area of the grounds. For culinary tidbits one might select from any number of wafting aromas - pasties, scones, or for the most brave – haggis. Haggis, a traditional Scottish dish and once a mainstay, is now considered an epicurean delicacy. The entrée traditionally is prepared with sheep or pig offal (one must wonder if the homonym is no coincidence) boiled in a sheep's stomach and mixed with oats and spices, although modern recipes can call for imitation ingredients for the more squeamish. If tasting this treat seems too *"Fear Factor*-ish" for the ordinary diner, there are numerous other delicacies to be had. In the midst of all the sights and smell to behold, the ears are busily digesting divergent sounds.

Snippets of tunes from the musicians converge from numerous directions. The audience can be treated to Celtic music in the traditional sense, humorous fashion, or even with rock flair. (For anyone who has never heard a jam performed on a bagpipe, it is an astonishing feat not to be missed.) One might be introduced to unfamiliar instruments such as a bodhran drum or a didgeridoo. Musicians are always eager to explain the histories of these instruments and give an auditory presentation. The lyrics hold the stories of Celtic lore - an entertaining and effective method to learn of great battles and the culture.

Nothing can compete with the majestic pipes of the Highlands however! The breathtaking sounds of mournful bagpipes and the accompanying rat-a-tat-tat of snare drums can be heard from every corner of the grounds. There is no shortage of lone pipers practicing their piece, where one hears the tuning of a bagpipe as a long discordant squeal as both the bags and the piper's lungs collect as much air as possible. After this initial cacophony, a recognized tune blasts forward at decibels unmatched for the size of the instrument. Bagpipes are often a love or hate relationship. For those who swear the sound touches the soul, it is likely the listener is also easily able to transport to an era when the mighty pipes signaled an impending battle when much before the first warrior, sword or horse was spotted on a battlefield, the mournful bellowing of the bagpipe preceded. Dazzling kilts, feathered hats and tams, decorative droning pipes and the beating of the drums often compel the crowd to stop in their tracks for the spectacular tattoo.

One can stroll by a vendor tent and pick up a broadsword for examination, and likely be taken aback by the effort it requires to lift these swords mere inches off the ground. It puts a new perspective on battle scenes, such as in *Braveheart*, where warriors wielded these swords above their heads as if they weighed as much as a broomstick. Browsing through bric-a-brac overflowing at each vendor stand reveals that practically anything is available - especially that with a clan design - from scarves, shirts and kilts to mouse pads, coffee mugs and jewelry, and more.

The clan tent area is a popular spot, where finding one's surname gives a sense of community and belonging. "*Clan*" means "children" and "*mac*" means "son of" in Scottish Gaelic, so Clan MacDonald, for example, would embrace "the children of the son of Donald" should one find their surname at their tent. One need not fear that their surname is not of Celtic origin, however, as the friendly folk open their arms to anyone willing to hear the proud retelling of their clan's history and join their clan's numbers. As *The Clan-Tent Cavaliers* explains there is no need to worry if a surname does not readily appear – there are more books that contain virtually every name, allowing you to claim a piece of Scotland regardless of your roots (The Clan-Tent Cavaliers, 1997). The attendee then receives an armful of clan literature, further strengthening this newly found connection.

 The Clan-Tent Cavaliers parodies the athletic fields with the telling of "loonies…pitching tree trunks at the ground" (The Clan-Tent Cavaliers, 1997). This refers to the *caber toss* event, which to an outsider does resemble precisely the line in the song. Lest someone think it really is an event of lunatics running around with precariously balanced 100-pound poles in the palms of their hands, all dressed in kilts no less, there is a method to the madness. All Highland events have a historical foundation. The games originated in early Scotland when clan chiefs held competitions to find the most worthy warriors and protectors of their clans (Rueb, 2007). The *caber toss* is a reenactment of castle invasions. Tree trunks would be hurled across moats or against castle walls. If hurled correctly, the trunk would hit the ground and turn end over end so that it would land precisely, enabling the warriors to cross the moat or scale the castle wall. Other athletic events include the hammer throw and the stone put. The *hammer throw* was a competition to test strength and often served the purpose of a "medieval job interview"; the most agile and strong winning the available job opening. The *stone put* competition probably requires the least amount of interpretation; simply, warriors tossed huge rocks in battle.

If still by this time nothing has particularly caught the attendee's attention, there remains even more to choose, from whiskey tasting to historical battle reenactments, or from Gaelic language lessons to perusing the living history section with its medieval arts and crafts. For the dancing aficionado one can either view Highland dancing (which like the athletic events has a history behind each step) or participate in Scottish country dancing, where volunteers are eager to teach basic cultural dance steps. The animal lover will be content watching the sheepherding dog exhibition or ambling through the barn area where the unusual appearances of Highland cattle and Irish wolfhounds call for more than a cursory glance.

With the abundance of wildly diverse things to see and do at a Scottish Highland Games, one would be hard-pressed to not enjoy some part of the event. It is difficult to attend only one Highland game. As *The Clan-Tent Cavaliers* fittingly states, *"We never miss a Highland Games, you'll always find us here. So come on in and sit you down, and have a drop of cheer. And we'll figure out a way of having you sit here next year!"* (The Clan-Tent Cavaliers, 1997)

Works Cited

Men of Worth (Performer). (1997). The Clan-Tent Cavaliers.
    On Live in Folsom. Mahog Music.
Rueb, E. S. (2007, September 7). Ahead|Highland Games;
    Testing the Power of the Plaid. New York Times, p. 2.

Highland Games

Diane Alexander

Highland Games are an eclectic mix of entertainment that offers something for everyone. The name can be somewhat misleading, as these festivities include not only competitive games but a diverse range of cultural events. Despite its growing popularity, the Highland Games themselves have still not been heard of by many; with even less knowing what constitutes "games." Notwithstanding the cultural backdrop attended by many of Celtic heritage, the demographics of the spectators are wide and varied.[1] What are Highland games and why have they become a popular spectator and tourist event in the United States? Almost all material written about Highland Games includes the word "community." And while community is a large draw to the games, the variety and enjoyment experienced when attending the games is the impetus to return. Take a virtual tour around a typical Highland Games. Developed from ancient times of warrior training and

---

[1] While Celtic heritage commonly denotes persons of Irish and Scottish heritage, Celts encompass much of the Indo-European family, including, but not limited to, Celts of Welsh, German, Scandinavian, Belgian, French, British, Spanish, Swiss, Hungarian, Portuguese, Italian, Austrian, Turkish, New Zealander, and Greek origins.

selections, perhaps no other entertainment forum offers as many varied activities, including food, drink, music, dancing, athletics, animal exhibitions, battle reenactments, living history exhibits, concerts and tattoos, crafts, shopping, and numerous cultural and history activities. One would be hard-pressed not to find one event that sparks an interest.

The modern Highland Games developed professionally in the early 1800s, although many of the events and athletics predate this more formal organization. There is evidence of games in colonial America as early as the eighteenth century. Until the nineteenth century, games held in North America were known as Caledonian Games (Gillespie, 2000). Its name came from the Roman word "Caledonia" which means northern Britain or Scotland. Caledonian societies were originally developed to provide assistance to immigrants from Scotland. Eventually they began incorporating other events into their society and celebrations, including the athletic games (caber toss, hammer throwing, and stone throwing) as well as music and Highland dancing (Gillespie, 2000).

Regardless of speculated precise origins of these games, the common thread is that they began as a competition to select the strongest warriors and to practice for warfare (Marjory Brewster, 2009). Although it is determined there is evidence of games before the Battle of Culloden, that event might well have provided a resurgence of nationalism when persons of Scottish ethnicity were forbidden by The Act of

Proscription, enacted in 1747, "1) the wearing of Highland dress, 2) the gathering of Highlanders, and 3) the carrying of official Highland weapons such as the targe, dirk, claymore and pistols (Doyle, 2006).[2] Other items, not specifically addressed by the Act, were forbidden following the Battle of Culloden, including banning bagpipes (considered an instrument of war) and the speaking of Gaelic by native Highlanders.

Highland Games, with its convergence of clans, kilts, weaponry and bagpipes, always open with great ceremony. The emcee or host, of the weekend and sometimes week-long festival, opens with a speech declaring the games officially under way. Games begin with a parade of the pipe and drum bands and each clan society that is represented at the games, carrying their clan banner and dressed in assorted items of their clan's plaid.[3] Many games also hold a *"kirking of the tartan"* – a church service blessing the tartan and in turn blessing all the clans and participants.[4]

Spectators have varying opinions to the most enthralling event of the games; however the vast majority of

---

[2] Targe: shield; dirk: small knife or dagger; claymore: large sword or broadsword. Highland dress includes wearing of the tartan or kilt. Tartan: woven plaid usually designed with a clan's design.

[3] Plaid: a clan's tartan, dress or design

[4] Kirk: Scottish form of "church". Clan: structure upon which many Celtic regions were organized, politically and socially, usually along familial lines.

respondents are divided between either the pipe and drum bands or the athletic competitions. Heading towards the athletic fields, the spectator will quickly determine this is not an ordinary playing field. A cursory glance around will reveal several people hoisting what looks like a telephone pole into the air, another person in a kilt swirling around in tight circles with fist pressed near the cheek, and yet another person swinging around and around with a long iron-looking object extended from the hands. These are the sights of unique sporting prowess – the "*heavy athletics.*"

Although the *caber toss* has several theories of origin, including house building and fertility rites, the most popular explanation is that the throwing of the caber is a reenactment of castle invasions and warfare. Tree trunks would be hurled across moats or against castle walls. If pitched correctly, the trunk would hit the ground and turn end over end, enabling the warriors to cross the moat or scale the castle wall. Although strength is important, there is a great deal of skill and technique to be employed as well. The caber is approximately 20 feet long and weighs an average of 100 pounds. Two people assist getting the caber upright for the competitor, who then grasps the caber, working his way down until he has it balanced and can cup it in the palms of his hands. He then lifts it up, balancing, and proceeds to move forward. Once the perfect balance and direction is attained (hopefully!), the competitor heaves the caber up and away from him. If it is a successful throw the caber will go up in the air, landing on one end, and then hovering until the forces of nature cause it to fall. If the caber properly lands end over end, i.e. at 180 degrees, the competitor is victorious.

The *hammer throw* was a competition to test strength and often served the purpose of a "medieval job interview", the most agile and strong winning the available job opening. The hammer is a replica of medieval blacksmiths' hammers and was used by workers in stone quarries. On average it weighs 20 pounds and is about four feet long. The competitor swings around in a circle two to three times and then releases the hammer. An alternative style is for the competitor to stand still and swing the hammer in a circle above the head until throwing it. The longest forward throw determines the victor.

The *weight over bar or weight throw* competition consists of heaving an approximate 30-60 pound iron weight with a chain and ring which the competitor grasps, over a bar resembling a high jump bar. This competition is believed to have begun with the training of throwing heavy grappling hooks up onto castle walls or other tall obstacles in order to scale the barriers. The competitor turns his back to the bar, grasps the weight, swinging it back and forth until the proper momentum is reached and hurls the weight over his shoulder and behind him, hopefully clearing the bar. The bar is continually raised until only one competitor remains, claiming victory.

The *stone throw* competition probably requires the least amount of interpretation; simply, warriors tossed huge rocks in battle. This can be likened to the modern *shot put* competition. The stone averages 20 pounds and is thrown from a standing position. And like the hammer throw, the longest distance determines the winner.

Spectators of the modern *highland dancing* competitions, consisting of almost all females (nearly 100 to 1), might be surprised to know that highland dancing was strictly only performed by males until the twentieth century (Doyle, 2006). The costume is the kilt (which presents somewhat of an anachronism as women never wore kilts in ancient Scotland.) As with other events in the Highland Games, highland dancing has its cultural and historical background.

The origins of highland dancing lie well beyond written material, passed down by oral tradition. What is known is that Scottish armies used the dancing as an exercise for soldiers to keep them in shape for battle. In "Introduction to Highland Dancing," it is remarked that the most common dance, the *Highland fling,* uses muscles from head to toe and the dancer jumps 192 times during the dance while performing intricate footwork (Duncan). It is not surprising it an excellent form of exercise. Highland dancing levels are similar to achieving karate belts – each performer must "pass" each level of increasing difficulty. These levels are beginner, novice, intermediate, and premier (Doyle, 2006).

The most commonly related history of the *Highland fling* is that it was a celebration dance when warriors returned home successfully from battle. The *Sword Dance* is thought to have been created by King Malcolm Canmore; purported that he laid swords in a cross over his slain enemy's body and danced a celebratory dance. Another common explanation is that soldiers danced the *Sword Dance* the night before a battle in a superstitious ritual. If the dancer touched the sword it was thought he might be wounded the next day, and if he kicked the sword it was believed he would be killed. The *Seann Triubhas* (pronounced shawn-trews and meaning "old trousers") was thought to have originated when the Act of Proscription was repealed in 1782, allowing the Scottish to wear their kilts again and shedding their hated trousers in celebration. The *Reel* is thought to have originated at church, where members would stomp their feet and clap their hands to keep warm until the minister arrived for services (Duncan).

David MacKenzie is quoted in "Skirling Pipes Swirling Kilts," stating, "Having once heard a massed pipe band, one feels this must be shared with the rest of the world" (Beld, 2007). *Pipe and drum bands* from far-reaching locales compete in every Highland Games festival. There are few spectators that are not stopped in their tracks when a parade of pipers and drummers marches by. The vast majority agree it is simply mesmerizing.

Competitions in bagpipes often include solo, band and pibroch (pronounced pea-brock.) Solo and band pieces are often referred to as the "lighter music", including jigs, reels, and marches. Pibroch is referred to as the "great music" or classical music of bagpipes. There are competition levels similar to highland dancing levels; only the numbering of levels goes from five to one, with one being the most difficult piping level.

The pipe band tattoo is a performance organized along soldier drill patterns. The tattoo, as described in the games program from the Antigonish Highland Games, comes from "incidences of drummers marching through the streets to issue a 'last call' to soldiers in taverns in Holland in the 17th century. The drum beat would signal the tavern-keepers to 'doe den tap toe' or 'turn off their taps.' This was eventually shortened to 'tap toe' and then became 'tattoo.'"

For culinary tidbits one might select from any number of wafting aromas - pasties, scones, or for the most brave – haggis. Haggis, a traditional Scottish dish and once a mainstay, is now considered an epicurean delicacy. The entrée traditionally is prepared with sheep or pig offal (one must wonder if the homonym is no coincidence) boiled in a sheep's stomach and mixed with oats and spices, although modern recipes can call for imitation ingredients for the more squeamish. If tasting this treat seems too *"Fear Factor*-ish" for the ordinary diner, there are numerous other delicacies to be had. There are neeps (turnips), often served with haggis, meat pies, shortbread, Irish soda bread and scones, among some of the more popular dishes.

Finding one's surname gives a sense of community and belonging. "*Clan*" means "children" and "*mac*" means "son of" in Scottish Gaelic, so Clan MacDonald, for example, would embrace "the children of the son of Donald" should one find their surname at their *clan tent*. There are usually 30-50 clans represented at each festival (Beld, 2007). While not every name can be found with Celtic origin, anybody is welcome to claim allegiance with the clan of their choosing; Clan Wallace gaining numerous new members with the popularity of the movie *Braveheart*, as an example.

The audience can be treated to Celtic music in the traditional sense, humorous fashion, or even with rock flair. (For anyone who has never heard a jam performed on a bagpipe, it is an astonishing feat not to be missed.) One might be introduced to unfamiliar instruments such as a bodhran or a didgeridoo.[5] Musicians are always eager to explain the histories of these instruments and give an auditory presentation. Many games hold a *ceilidh* (pronounced kay-lee) at the end of their games. A ceilidh is Scottish Gaelic for party

---

[5] Bodhran: a small hand-held drum often made of goatskin. Didgeridoo: a woodwind instrument of Australian aborigines.

or get-together. Typically all the musicians from the festival perform at the ceilidh and there is usually food and beer or ale.

There are vendors present at every festival, offering clan dress articles, weaponry, musical items, jewelry, paintings, clothing, souvenirs and crafts. The animal lover can watch the sheepherding dog exhibition or amble through the barn area, where the unusual appearances of Highland cattle and Irish wolfhounds call for more than a cursory glance. And in the unlikely event nothing has sparked the interest of the spectator, there remains a plethora of events to choose from depending on the individualized programs found at each event, including: poetry readings, living history areas, battle reenactments, Frisbee dogs, Clydesdale horses, car shows, whiskey tasting, "Bonniest Knees" contests, haggis tasting and Gaelic lessons.

In Erin Doyle's "The Community is the Culture," a Highland Games host is quoted at the closing ceremonies, "The closing rite is symmetrical to the opening one, marks the end of the festive activities and the return to the normal spatial and temporal dimensions of daily life" (Doyle, 2006). As much excitement as is teeming at the opening ceremonies, there appears to be as much sadness and nostalgia abounding at the closing ceremonies. Highland Games are a wonderful method in which to reconnect with the historical past. It is rare to find a participant or spectator who can only attend one game and have no interest to ever attend one again. It is certainly one of the most diverse entertainment forums in existence, where all can "…be transported – in spirit at least – across the Atlantic to the Highlands and islands of Scotland" (Beld, 2007).

Bibliography
Beld, G. G. (2007, May/June). Skirling Pipes Swirling Kilts.
      Michigan History.
Doyle, E. (2006). The community is the culture (Dissertation,
      Newfoundland, Canada, 2005.) Masters Abstracts
      International.
Duncan, K. (n.d.). Introduction to Highland Dancing.
      Retrieved December 5, 2009, from Electric Scotland:
      http://www.electricscotland.com/dance/intro.htm
Gillespie, G. (2000). Roderick McLennan, Professionalism,
      and the Emergence of the Athlete in Caledonian
      Games. Sport History Review , 31, 43-63.
Marjory Brewster, J. C. (2009, May). The Scottish Highland
      Games: evolution, development and role as a
      community event. Current Issues in Tourism , 271-293.
Neville, G. K. (1979). Community Form and Ceremonial Life
      in Three Regions of Scotland. American Ethnologist , 6
      (1), 93-109.

Links to bibliographic articles:
Beld, G. G. (2007, May/June). Skirling pipes swirling Kilts.
      Michigan History.
http://ezproxy.umuc.edu/login?url=http://search.ebscohost.com
      /login.aspx?direct=true&db=ahl&AN=A800031135.01
      &loginpage=login.asp&site=ehost-live&scope=site
Doyle, E. (2006). The community is the culture (Dissertation,
      Newfoundland, Canada, 2005.) Masters Abstracts
      International.
http://ezproxy.umuc.edu/login?url=http://search.ebscohost.com
      /login.aspx?direct=true&db=ahl&AN=A700019801.01
      &loginpage=login.asp&site=ehost-live&scope=site
Duncan, K. (n.d.). Introduction to highland dancing. Retrieved
      December 5, 2009, from Electric Scotland:
      http://www.electricscotland.com/dance/intro.htm
Gillespie, G. (2000). Roderick McLennan, professionalism,
      and the emergence of the athlete in Caledonian games.
      Sport History Review , 31, 43-63.

http://ezproxy.umuc.edu/login?url=http://search.ebscohost.com
/login.aspx?direct=true&db=ahl&AN=A000489768.01
&loginpage=login.asp&site=ehost-live&scope=site

Marjory Brewster, J. C. (2009, May). The Scottish highland
games: evolution, development and role as a
community event. Current Issues in Tourism , 271-293.

http://ezproxy.umuc.edu/login?url=http://search.ebscohost.com
/login.aspx?direct=true&db=eoah&AN=18848473&log
inpage=login.asp&site=ehost-live&scope=site

Neville, G. K. (1979). Community form and ceremonial life in
three regions of Scotland. American Ethnologist , 6 (1),
93-109.

http://ezproxy.umuc.edu/login?url=http://search.ebscohost.com
/login.aspx?direct=true&db=mzh&AN=1979116175&l
oginpage=login.asp&site=ehost-live&scope=site

Coca-Colonization: How the Invention of Coca-Cola Changed the World

Diane Alexander

When the Berlin Wall fell, one of the first western consumer products sampled by East Germans was Coca-Cola. Before this event, Coca-Cola had been banned in many eastern European countries, accused among other things of being an imperialist symbol and a poison. Shortly following the demise of the Berlin Wall, Coca-Cola had bottling plants in East Germany. Being on the ground at this auspicious time resulted in today's remarkable market share of Coke products in many European countries, leaving its competitors in the dust. Coca-Colonization has its place in global vernacular and marketing right alongside Americanization and McDonaldization.[1] Today, it is theorized that Coca-Cola is the second-most recognized phrase around the globe, trailing only the word "okay."[2]

---

[1] Jerry H. Bentley and Herbert F. Ziegler, Traditions & Encounters: A Global Perspective on the Past, Fifth Edition, Volume 2, New York: McGraw-Hill, 2011, 901.

[2] 125 Years of Sharing Happiness," The Coca-Cola Company. March 30, 2011, http://assets.coca-colacompany.com/7b/46/e5be4e7d43488c2ef43ca1120a15/TCCC_1 25Years_Booklet_Spreads_Hi.pdf (accessed April 9, 2013).

At first blush, Coca-Cola does not appear to be a technology in itself. Inventions and innovation are often responsible for making life easier or increasing productivity. Oftentimes, they are credited with changing the world. The invention of Coca-Cola did not result in streamlining work procedures or speeding up a process, yet, it certainly changed the world in certain respects. The invention and development of Coca-Cola follows a more unusual path than many of its significant counterparts. How did this humble invention, originally created as a patent medicine, follow its auspicious beginnings in Atlanta, Georgia in 1886 to become one of the most firmly entrenched pieces of Americana and global icon? Coca-Cola is one of the most incredible and unusual story of technology of any modern invention.

Coca-Cola takes its rare place as the most significant, yet perhaps one of the least needed, technologies of all. It holds many records, among such as having the oldest, most closely guarded trade secret, known as formula 7X. Throughout its path of invention, technology, and innovation of secret recipes, controversial ingredients, altering ingredients while retaining the original flavor, technology and innovation of bottling and bottle design, innovation in distribution, technology of marketing and advertising, and the technology and innovation of consumerism and pop culture, Coca-Cola has become one of the most recognized and influential products around the globe. No other technology can state it provided so little as far as a necessary or required product and yet had so much impact in globalization and Americana.

It might seem as if Coca-Cola should never have gotten off the ground. Coca-Cola had a fractious beginning and charted a somewhat unpredictable path and outcome from its inception. Invented in 1884 by Dr. John Stith Pemberton, an Atlanta pharmacist, it was initially called French Wine Coca and it contained cocaine, caffeine, and alcohol, among its ingredients. In 1885, the Temperance Movement was in full swing and Atlanta banned the sale of alcohol. Pemberton had only to remove the alcohol to continue hawking his product, as cocaine was not banned until 1914.[3] Pemberton sold the rights of Coca-Cola to Asa Candler. At the time Candler held the reins of Coca-Cola, the company became no stranger to legal battles. Not only did Coca-Cola prevail in all its cases, but it also forever changed regulations and law within corporations and the federal government, including the Internal Revenue Service and Food and Drug Administration, and marketing regulations and procedures.[4]

In 1900, Coca-Cola sued the Internal Revenue Service (Coca Cola Co. vs. Henry Rucker, IRS Tax Commissioner,

---

[3] The Coca-Cola Company, 2013, http://www.coca-colacompany.com/ (accessed April 9, 2013).

[4] Ann Uhry Abrams, Formula for Fortune: How Asa Candler Discovered Coca-Cola and Turned It into the Wealth His Children Enjoyed, Bloomington, IN: iUniverse, 2012, 68.

1900) to remove the tax on the product. The IRS taxed Coca-Cola as a medicinal product. Coca-Cola successfully sued, stating Coca-Cola was a fountain drink, not a medicine and the IRS unsuccessfully appealed the case.[5] By 1906, cocaine had been removed from the beverage, leaving the decocainized coca leaves. To avoid bad publicity, Coca-Cola took the lead and attached testimonials to their advertising. One such ad from 1906, hailing Coca-Cola as "The Great National Temperance Beverage," included a statement from a state chemist who testified he had examined the beverage and found no evidence of cocaine.[6] In 1906, Harvey Wiley was appointed the first commissioner of the Food and Drug Administration. His organization began prosecuting companies that sold products with harmful ingredients and Coca-Cola was on Wiley's radar. The trial was known by several idiomatic names, including The Poison Brain Tonic Trial and the Great Coke Trial of 1911. Even its official case name sounds colloquial: United States v. Forty Barrels and Twenty Kegs of Coca Cola, The Coca-Cola Company of Atlanta, Georgia.[7]

---

[5] The U.S. National Archives and Records Administration," National Archives,
http://www.archives.gov/research/arc/topics/courts.html (accessed April 24, 2013).

[6] The World of Coca-Cola, 2013, http://www.worldofcoca-cola.com (accessed April 9, 2013).

[7] Mark Pendergrast, For God, Country and Coca-Cola: The Definitive History of the Great American Soft Drink and the Company that Makes It, New York: Basic Books, 1993, 116.

Oddly enough, Wiley did not intercept the shipment because of allegations of cocaine but rather because of caffeine. Wiley testified caffeine was a harmful, toxic product that was habit-forming. He sued Coca-Cola on the basis that caffeine, a toxic stimulant, was added to the drink, and that the product was sold to children. Coca-Cola successfully proved that that caffeine was not added to the drink, but rather was a natural occurring essential component of Coke. The case was dismissed and the government appealed. There was an out-of-court settlement reached during the appeals period, during which Coca-Cola voluntarily reduced the amount of caffeine in the product.[8] This would be the last change to the formula of the infamous and controversial drink until 1985 with the introduction of New Coke.

Despite all the legal battles and discovery of trial documents endured, Coca-Cola still managed to keep 7X top secret. Candler believed many of the court battles were an attempt to obtain the secret recipe. The introduction of New Coke, and subsequent return to Classic Coke was one of the watershed moments in Coca-Cola's history, indicating the sum of the parts were greater than the whole. It was a colossal failure and a black mark in Coca-Cola's history. Coca-Cola was much more than a humble invention in a pharmacist's workroom. It was a part of American culture, and changing it

---

[8] Pendergrast, For God, Country and Coca-Cola, 116-119.

in any way, despite the modern visions of current board members and corporate officials, resulted in a fierce and unexpected consumer uproar. Sufficiently scolded, Coca-Cola eliminated New Coke within the next couple of years. The lesson learned for Coca-Cola was not all technology needs be changed or altered.

Coca-Cola spawned numerous cultural changes. In addition to corporate law, taxes, and federal regulations, Coca-Cola changed global marketing and advertising and helped shape the modern day image of consumerism. With more than 50 slogans – about one every couple of years since its inception – Coca-Cola has paved the way for successful advertising and globalization. Moreover, it has done more than lead the way with catchy taglines and advertising dollars spent. Coca-Cola has managed to effectively weave its way into American fabric and succeed in what only a handful of other products have been able to accomplish – to convince consumers it is not about buying a product but rather it is owning a part of the feeling, nostalgia, and history of Coca-Cola. From slogans and taglines, to the 1970s hilltop singing of "I'd Like to Teach the World to Sing," to Mean Joe Greene commercials, to a cheerful makeover of Santa Claus, to whimsical polar bears, Coca-Cola has paved not only the way in successful marketing but has proven that you can sell an idea as well as an object. In addition to its many achievements, Coca-Cola holds notable fame in philanthropy, sponsorship of minorities, and environmental sustainability. No small list of accomplishments for such a simplistic soft drink with modest beginnings.

In his article "The Church of Baseball, the Fetish of Coca-Cola, and the Potlatch of Rock 'n' Roll," David Chidester likens the status of baseball, Coca-Cola, and rock 'n roll in Americana to religious fervor and fetishes. Chidester details aspects of these three American icons, noting the dedication to these as somewhat remarkable, particularly considering all three are leisure activities, non-necessary for survival or benefit, and yet difficult to imagine American life without. As to Coca-Cola's success and elevation to a "religion," a glimpse into Coca-Cola's marketing approach is gained with company president Robert Goizuieta's statement, "Our success will largely depend on the degree to which we make it impossible for the consumer around the globe to escape Coca-Cola."[9] This provides insight as to Coca-Cola's stratagem since inception: convince the consumer that they both want and need this product. The strategy of keeping Coca-Cola within arm's length is significantly illustrated with Coca-Cola's role in wars, namely World War II and the Cold War.

A watershed in Coca-Cola's solid foothold in Americana occurred during World War II, a war known for its innovation and technological weapons. How was Coca-Cola on

---

[9] (Chidester 1996), 751.

the front lines, taking up valuable cargo space right alongside armor, weapons, and food? Having survived the Great Depression, Coca-Cola, like numerous other companies, found itself in a tough business environment. Sales and consumerism were depressed. The only way to increase business was to do so overseas, but the cost of providing Coca-Cola to the military was exorbitant. Robert Woodruff, CEO of Coca-Cola from 1923 to 1954, insisted cost be damned - he wanted every military member to be able to have a Coke for five cents no matter where stationed. Woodruff's seemingly simple goal was not simple in the least. Cargo space was precious and expensive and needed for weaponry and food. Additionally, the problem of returning the bottles to the United States existed. Coca-Cola's solution was to build bottling plants overseas to provide the front lines with "America's soft drink." When Eisenhower surveyed troops, surprisingly he found that soldiers would rather have Coca-Cola than beer. The company went to work securing wartime contracts, and shortly after, Coca-Cola was awarded priority shipping.[10]

Many objected. Some military officials protested, claiming it would take up valuable needed transport space. Pepsi objected, stating Coca-Cola would have a monopoly. What no one expected was the "gush of raw emotion that

---

[10] Frederick Allen, Secret Formula: How Brilliant Marketing and Relentless Salesmanship Made Coca-Cola the Best-Known Product in the World, New York: Harper Business, 1994, 254-255.

Coca-Cola aroused in the American armies…The familiar bottle and trademark and taste turned out to be a poignant reminder of home for hundreds of thousands and eventually millions of young soldiers who found themselves in strange places facing terrible danger."[11] Despite all the objections and wrangling to provide the troops with Coca-Cola, it demonstrated that there was a profound longing and attachment for Coca-Cola, one writer noting, "Soldiers wanted four things from home: mail, cigarettes, chewing gum, and Coke."[12] Newspapers filled with pictures of soldiers holding bottles of Coke.

The press coverage was not limited to the United States. The enemy noticed also, and propagandized that Coca-Cola was evil, a poison, and an imperialist symbol. Japanese press reported, "With Coca-Cola we imported the germs of a disease from American society."[13] The negative press would continue throughout the Cold War. Communists believed the company doubled as a spy network and warned about the dangers of the Coca-Colonization of Europe. Axis nations tried to get it banned as a poison. It remains banned in only two countries today: North Korea and Cuba. It is phenomenal that a humble invention, that no one really needs, played such a huge role in wars, standing toe-to-toe alongside remarkable

---

[11] Allen, Secret Formula, 257.

[12] Allen, Secret Formula, 257.

[13] Pendergrast, For God, Country and Coca-Cola, 208.

twentieth-century inventions, holding itself up as a beacon of western culture. Pemberton would have been stunned to see the results of his invention.

Coca-Cola survived legal battles over contentious ingredients, the Great Depression, wars, and stiff competition from Pepsi-Cola. A German press chief might have grumbled, "America never contributed anything to world civilization but chewing gum and Coca-Cola, " but what a worldwide contribution the invention of Coca-Cola did provide.[14] From its first decades of cutthroat and contentious legal battles, to marketing the unique and instantly recognizable Coke bottle, to becoming the second most well-known phrase in the world, the technology of Coca-Cola has followed a phenomenal path. While it did influence the technology of cold beverages and the bottling process in certain respects, and spawn innovation in the beverage industry, its true innovative impact can be seen in by its role in pop culture, marketing, and advertising, governmental images, wars, and even iconic polar bears and Santa Claus! Regardless of its success in retaining an economic hold in the global marketplace, Coca-Cola will forever be enshrined in Americana. Coca-Cola proves that the narrative of technology is not always a common and predictable one. The technology of Coca-Cola is certainly an outlier in its unique

---

[14] Pendergrast, For God, Country and Coca-Cola, 208.

history, proving that not all technology need be purely physical, scientific, and necessary.

BIBLIOGRAPHY

"125 Years of Sharing Happiness." The Coca-Cola Company. March 30, 2011. http://assets.coca-colacompany.com/7b/46/e5be4e7d43488c2ef43ca1120a15/TCCC_125Years_Booklet_Spreads_Hi.pdf (accessed April 9, 2013).

Abrams, Ann Uhry. Formula For Fortune: How Asa Candler Discovered Coca-Cola And Turned It Into The Wealth His Children Enjoyed. Bloomington, IN: iUniverse, 2012.

Allen, Frederick. Secret Formula: How Brilliant Marketing and Relentless Salesmanship Made Coca-Cola the Best-Known Product in the World. New York: Harper Business, 1994.

Bentley, Jerry H., and Herbert F. Ziegler. Traditions & Encounters: A Global Perspective on the Past, Fifth Edition, Volume 2. New York: McGraw-Hill, 2011.

Chidester, David. "The Church of Baseball, the Fetish of Coca-Cola, and the Potlatch of Rock 'n' Roll: Theoretical Models for the Study of Religion in American Popular Culture." Journal of the American Academy of Religion 64, no. 4 (Winter 1996): 743-765.

Gieryn, Thomas F. "Science and Coca-Cola." Science & Technology Studies (Sage Publications, Inc.) 5, no. 1 (Spring 1987): 12-21+31.

Pendergrast, Mark. For God, Country and Coca-Cola: The Definitive History of the Great American Soft Drink and the Company that Makes It. New York: Basic Books, 1993.

The Coca-Cola Company. 2013. http://www.coca-colacompany.com/ (accessed April 9, 2013).

"The U.S. National Archives and Records Administration." National Archives. http://www.archives.gov/research/arc/topics/courts.html (accessed April 24, 2013).

The World of Coca-Cola. 2013. http://www.worldofcoca-cola.com/ (accessed April 9, 2013).

Young, James Harvey. "Three Southern Food and Drug
    Cases." The Journal of Southern History (Southern
    Historical Association) 49, no. 1 (February 1983): 3-36.

Divided Familial Loyalties in the Civil War

Diane Alexander

> "Two brothers on their way,
> One wore blue, and one wore gray."
> - *"Two Brothers" by Irving Gordon*

"Brother against brother" is a term that not only described the North and South citizens divided in the Civil War, but also is a deeper symbolic phrase that represented families at odds with each other – brother against brother, father against son, siblings and in-laws against each other, and even wives against husbands. As the nation divided, so did many families, as they grappled with divided loyalties and conflicting ideologies on the home front. Many families fought a war on two fronts.

The ideal of the model family evolved from the American Revolution, with aspects of Republican motherhood and raising ideal citizens for the nation complementing the model. Joan Cashin in "The War Was You and Me: Civilians in the American Civil War" asserts, "Society viewed the family as the bedrock of society."[1] Aaron Sheehan-Dean states in

"Why Confederates Fought," that, "Historians have demonstrated that during this period men came to value intimate family relations as the highest goal of life, or at least as worthy a goal as participation in the political and economic spheres."[2] These cohesive, honorable, and loyal units were not meant to divide; but then again, the country was not meant to divide either. With the family unit held in such high societal esteem, it is little wonder that the Civil War rent asunder not only the United States, but also the foundation of its society: the family unit.

Despite countless accounts of bitter protestations of disownment, fierce and angry accusations, and highly contentious situations that tore rifts in many families, Amy Murrell Taylor, "The Divided Family in Civil War America," claims that many families never simply abandoned each other, even at the beginning of the war, regardless of the existence of conflicting ideologies within the home front.[3] This was particularly true of border state families, where much of the most gruesome and grueling battles occurred, driving home the

---

[1] Joan E. Cashin, *The War Was You and Me: Civilians in the American Civil War* (Princeton: Princeton University Press, 2002), 358.

[2] Aaron Sheehan-Dean, *Why Confederates Fought: Family and Nation in Civil War Virginia*, (ReadHowYouWant.com, 2009), xxiv.

[3] Amy Murrell Taylor, *The Divided Family in Civil War* (University of North Carolina Press, 2005), 154.

devastation and tragedy of war. Regardless of political and ideological chasms, the knowledge alone of the possibility that their relatives were being maimed and killed helped outweigh even the strongest of disapproval and professed disownment of certain family members.

Although post-war reconciliation is much harder to trace and prove, as the wartime letters and correspondence expressing diverse sentiments and ideologies ceased, many accounts do exist that allow a view of the varied reconciliation processes or even the unfortunate eternal divisions.[4] The term reconciliation, itself, has varying degrees and is subject to interpretation. As Taylor states, "If reconciliation meant a return to status quo, a resumption of the same conversations, activities, and feelings they had shared in peacetime, then divided families never reconciled."[5] However, this is true of united families as well. The Civil War did not bring a status quo to anyone and for the most part, drastically altered the structures of mentality, mindsets, and family life and activities. Taylor further explains reconciliation was a complex procedure, and the initial gestures of assistance and economic aid were often much easier and came quicker than the emotional components of forgiveness and understanding.[6]

---

[4] Taylor, *The Divided Family*, 165.
[5] Taylor, *The Divided Family*, 153.
[6] Taylor, *The Divided Family*, 153.

It is difficult to ascertain a predictable pattern in families whose loyalties divided. Studies and surveys have attempted to collect certain demographical information in antebellum America to determine patterns and statistics, such as birthplace and longevity of residence. However, the best that can be garnered from this information is common patterns, but never predictable. In divisions between father and son, the predominant pattern was the Unionist father and the Rebel son. A historical backdrop illustrates why this is so. Firstly, it was older generation vs. younger generation; the generation gap eternally responsible for more division in a family than any other factor. Secondly, fathers in antebellum America often tended to be more moderate, and in favor of compromise, especially toward secessionist views. Josie Underwood of Bowling Green, Kentucky, wrote in a letter a common shared sentiment, "all the men...of any position or prominence whatever are Union men – and yet many of these men have wild reckless unthinking inexperienced sons who make so much noise about secession as to almost drown their fathers wiser council."[7] Some historians of secession have theorized that younger generations were more in favor of secession because of the patriotic causes upon which they were reared. On the heels of the American Revolution, the younger

---

[7] David Williams, *Bitterly Divided: The South's Inner Civil War*, (New York: The New Press, 2010), 45.

generation was nourished upon the ideals of liberty and freedom – precisely these Republican ideals.[8]

Brother against brother, literally, was more common than some Civil War material might imply. Countless families, even notable or prominent ones, were afflicted with some degree of division. Mary Todd Lincoln had four brothers and three brothers-in-law (one a general) in the Confederate army.[9] Of the Todd family sons, only one served in the Union. Of the Todd family daughters, five were loyal to the Union and four supported the Confederacy. Among other political families affected by a familial division were the Clay, Crittenden, and Breckinridge families.

During the Civil War, there were sometimes "close calls" with unknown participants in battle against each other, such as the Campbell and Prentiss brothers. Alexander and James Campbell unknowingly fought each other at the Battle of James Island (or the Battle of Secession), both fortuitously in the same area but missing each other by a slim margin of time. Clifton and William Prentiss also unknowingly battled each other, both wounded within minutes and yards of each other.

---

[8] Cashin, *The War Was You and Me*, 365.

[9] James M. McPherson and James K. Hogue, *Ordeal by Fire: The Civil War and Reconstruction*, (Boston: McGraw-Hill, 2009), 168.

James and Alexander Campbell, along with their siblings, emigrated from Scotland to the United States in the 1850s. They were teenagers at the time, and part of the family settled in New York and part of them in South Carolina. Alexander was a stonecutter in New York; however, he worked as a stonemason in Charleston shortly before the war. He joined a local predominantly Scottish volunteer militia group in Charleston, and then upon return to his New York home, he enlisted in the 79th Regiment, New York State Militia. James was a drayman in Charleston who enlisted in the Union Light Infantry, also called the Scotch Company or the Charleston Highlanders, another predominantly Scottish volunteer militia. The antebellum volunteer militia groups were often social groups of similar heritage and culture members, and neither brother probably imagined these groups would prepare them for an upcoming war.[10]

With both brothers in their Highlander regiments on the eve of war, they were aware of their opposed sides of the cause, yet continued to correspond with each other. Their regiments placed them within miles of each other when the war initially began in Charleston. When Alexander heard from a

---

[10] Terry A. Johnston, Alexander Campbell, and James Campbell, *Him on the One Side and Me on the Other: The Civil War Letters of Alexander Campbell, 79th New York Infantry Regiment and James Campbell, 1st South Carolina Battalion*, (Charleston: University of South Carolina Press, 1999), 4-5.

captured prisoner that his brother, James, was fighting near James Island, he wrote his wife, summarizing the subtitle for the Civil War aptly, "We are not far from each other now…a warr [sic] that there never was the like of before Brother against Brother."[11]

At the time of the First Battle of James Island, also known as the Battle of Secessionville, on June 16, 1862, James and Alexander unwittingly faced each other. Alexander, a Color Sergeant, was responsible for planting the United States flag before the parapet at the fort in Secessionville, defending it until ordered otherwise. James, a Confederate lieutenant, climbed the same parapet later in the battle, and fought from the same area in which his brother had planted the flag. It was not until sometime after the battle that the brothers became aware of exactly how close they had been to each other in battle. Upon discovering this, James wrote Alexander, expressing his surprise and hoping that they would never again meet face to face on the battlefield. Should this occur, however, James assured Alexander that they both must do their duty for their cause and country.[12] According to Johnston, this letter was carried across James Island under a truce flag. The

---

[11] Johnston et al, *Him on the One Side*, 92.

[12] William J. Hamilton, III, "Brother Against Brother at Secessionville," *Civil War Preservation Trust*, (2009) http://www.civilwar.org/battlefields/secessionville/secessionville-history-articles/brother-against-brother-at.html. Web. 16 Nov. 2010.

Charleston Courier wrote an article about the battle, highlighting the brothers' actions, stating that each had served his cause with honor and courage, yet it was an "illustration of the deplorable consequences of this fratricidal war."[13]

In April 1863, Alexander resigned his commission because of lingering problems from a gunshot wound in 1862 and returned to his home in New York. In July 1863, James was taken prisoner and remained in prison until the end of the war. After his release, he returned to Charleston. Alexander and James continued to correspond throughout and after the war. Correspondence between these two, including letters James wrote from prison, illuminates many aspects of the fraternal aspects of the war. Johnston states, "Although these two men held divergent ideological and political beliefs and soldiered on opposing sides of a vigorously fought struggle, the familial bond that linked Alexander and James Campbell not only survived the Civil War but was apparently strengthened by it."[14] Both brothers survived the war and did well for themselves afterward. John Taylor in "Sibling Rivalry" observes, "Paradoxically, it was James, in the defeated South, who became a landowner of consequence."[15]

---

[13] Hamilton, "Brother Against Brother."

[14] Johnston et al, *Him on the One Side*, xiii.

[15] John M. Taylor, "Sibling Rivalry," *Civil War Times* 38, no. 5 (1999): 65. Academic OneFile. Web. 5 Dec. 2010.

The Prentiss brothers did not fare as well as the Campbell brothers. Clifton Kennedy Prentiss and William Scollay Prentiss were native Baltimoreans. Clifton became a Union soldier and William joined the Confederate army. According to Kevin Walsh, in "Forgotten New York: Views of a Lost Metropolis," Clifton was shocked when his brother joined the rebel cause and swore he would never talk to his brother again.[16] David H. Jones immortalized their story in his book, "Two Brothers: One North, One South," choosing to write it in historical fiction format to receive a larger readership. Although historical fiction is usually shunned in the scholastic field, the book was based upon actual events, confirmed by numerous sources, and is worthy of inclusion as an important source of divided families in the Civil War. Jones chose the genre in order to have a larger readership, stating, "After all, the circumstance of 'brother fighting brother' is the quintessential story of the Civil War."[17] He believed that both these brothers were American patriots, descendants of Revolution War patriots, and although they were divided in their ideologies, the nation's history should be honored by acquiring a better understanding of it.[18]

---

[16] Kevin Walsh, *Forgotten New York: Views of a Lost Metropolis* (New York, NY: Harpers Collins, 2006), xlvii.

[17] David H. Jones, *Two Brothers: One North, One South*, Staghorn Press, 2008.

[18] Jones, *Two Brothers*.

Walt Whitman was one of many contributors to the Prentiss brothers' story, having served as an aide in a Union hospital where both brothers were hospitalized on the same day. Several members of Clifton Kennedy's regiment also wrote memoirs, including the fateful day when both brothers fell on the battlefield. Although numerous variations exist of exactly how they were wounded and their reactions upon seeing each other, what is known is that they were both taken to the same Sixth Corps hospital.[19]

Both brothers were soldiering in the Petersburg campaign. Major Clifton Kennedy Prentiss was in charge of a regiment from the 6th Maryland. Leading his troops, he climbed a parapet, and a rifle ball struck him, tearing away part of his breastbone. Private William Scollay Prentiss of Lee's army suffered a traumatic injury within minutes of his brother on the morning of April 2, 1865. His injury would require amputation of his leg. According to the memoirs of Sergeant John R. King, when some Union men were tending to the wounded on the battlefield and came to William, he asked if they knew of Captain Clifton K. Prentiss. They replied affirmatively, stating Prentiss was now a major and he was lying wounded on the battlefield as well. William asked to see him, but purportedly when Clifton received this message, he

---

[19] A. Wilson Greene, *The Final Battles of the Petersburg Campaign: Breaking the Backbone of the Rebellion*, (University of Tennessee Press, 2008), 242.

denied his brother's request, stating, "I want to see no man who fired on my country's flag."[20] According to King, Clifton was eventually persuaded, and when William was laid beside him, he glared at him, but after William smiled, the two brothers reached out hands to each other, crying. It was an ironic and traumatic fate that brought these divided brothers together after having fought on bitterly opposed sides for more than three years.

Walt Whitman relates some of their stories from the hospital. He talks of his time in the hospital, administering whatever comfort possible to the patients. He writes of the night he stayed beside William's bedside. William's leg was amputated and he was on a high dose of morphine. When Whitman consoled him and held his hand, William stated he likely did not know who he was – a Confederate soldier. Whitman stated that no, he did not know that, but it did not matter to him. He stayed with William for the next two weeks, as he lingered on the brink of death, finally succumbing to his wounds in June 1865. Whitman writes also of visiting the next ward in which William's brother, Clifton was hospitalized. Like William, Clifton was lingering in death, succumbing to his wounds in August of that same year. The day after William's death, Clifton, Whitman, and John Melville were having a conversation in Clifton's ward. Speaking about

____

²⁰ Greene, *The Final Battles*, 241.

Southerners and their lost cause, Clifton stated, "I have no doubt that many remained steadfast in their convictions and dedication. And that included our brother William."[21] Whitman stated, "He never wavered in his loyalty to the Southern cause, his fellow soldiers or his dear friends in Richmond" to which Clifton replied, "I can only respect him for that."[22] Whitman would later note their bittersweet fraternal relationship in that both had fought for their cause, both had been seriously wounded, both had been brought together after a four-year separation, and both had died for their cause. Jones writes that despite their different causes, "[T]hey were able to reconcile their personal differences before the extent of their wounds proved fatal."[23]

Although brother against brother appears to be the most common of opposed family members, perhaps the most contentious and divisive of situations was father against son. While there were no predictable patterns, the most common was that of Unionist father against Rebel son. This went against the nineteenth-century family ideal even more so than brother against brother did.

Often the "ostracized" member of the family would attempt to provide for his family from afar, including sending money, smuggling goods, food, and medicine.[24] This often

---

[21] Jones, *Two Brothers*.

[22] Jones, *Two Brothers*.

[23] Jones, *Two Brothers*.

served multiple purposes – to prove loyalty to family despite differences, to assuage conscience for taking a different stance than other familial members, particularly the father figure, and/or to prove that both honor and a cause could be defended, but family remained the top priority. Although many continued to fight for the cause they believed in, they demonstrated that when all was said and done, the familial bond was of utmost importance to protect.

Brutus J. Clay was a Unionist, Whig leader, and member of the Kentucky legislature. His brother, Cassius Clay, was an outspoken abolitionist. His son, Ezekiel (Zeke), secretly planned his enlistment in the Confederate army. Zeke's brother, Christopher, also joined the Confederate cause. Distant relatives in this family exhibited the same division. These Kentucky Clays were distant cousins to Henry Clay, an abolitionist and prominent Whig leader, who himself had three grandsons in the Union and four in the Confederacy.[25]

Both Clay brothers kept their families foremost in their minds while fighting for their cause. It was common for "letters of protection" to be sent when known that an opposing side would raid near a soldier's home. This was usual, particularly in Border States. Christopher Clay wrote a letter to his family warning of a raid by Confederate Kirby Smith in Kentucky in 1862. He advised them to bury all the silver and to

---

[24] Taylor, *The Divided Family,* 155.

[25] McPherson, *Ordeal by Fire,* 167.

be careful, as the troops would attempt to take Brutus as a "hostage." He assured his family that he and Zeke would have a friend keep an eye out for the family. This written warning apparently succeeded, since the Clays were not raided and Brutus remained unharmed. In addition to warning his family to keep them safe, Christopher felt he had disproved his father's accusations of abandoning his filial duties and vows of familial protection when he joined the Confederacy. Apparently, Brutus did not hold as much esteem in his son's efforts, stating to his wife, "all the protection I need from my rebel son is to shoot the rogues who come to steal."[26] Like many Unionist fathers, Brutus was skeptical about his sons' true loyalties and their "fanatical" reasons for fighting the Confederate cause.

The Union had a policy to parole Confederate prisoners, although this was not used haphazardly. There were many hoops to jump through, and rather than simply forcing the prisoner to issue an oath (which could be easily revoked upon release), the family had to vouch for the prisoner. In a certain way, the Union controlled an advantageous political marketing campaign, presuming these Union families would work hard at converting the rebel family members, who would ultimately pledge allegiance to the Union. Taylor states the most common usage of this policy was Union fathers who had

---

[26] Cashin, *The War Was You and Me*, 379.

Confederate sons imprisoned. Making comparisons to the Bible and fatherly authority, these wayward sons would be forgiven for their sins and returned to homes where, undoubtedly under fatherly influence and authority, they would see the errors of their ways.[27]

Some fathers laid down strict criteria, making the son proved he was truly repentant. Other fathers refused to attempt to parole their sons, believing their contrition to be unreal, not trusting them to remain faithful to their oath of allegiance, or some simply believing imprisonment the best thing for their welfare, as they were fed, clothed, and away from battle. The paternal influence does not infer sons did not have a say in these matters. Some preferred to remain in prison, loyal to their cause and beliefs and unwilling to betray their loyalty to the cause. Zeke Clay was one such example.

While imprisoned, Zeke refused his father's help to parole him. He believed parole would mark him as a traitor and deserter, and he would rather remain imprisoned than swear allegiance to the Union. Brutus, despite his initial insistence of disowning his sons, understood his son's adherence to loyalty, stating to his daughter, "I would certainly not wish him to do anything that was dishonorable."[28] Despite his son's independence and refusal for help, when Zeke was finally released and returned home, it was upon terms that Brutus

---

[27] Taylor, *The Divided Family*, 160.

[28] Taylor, *The Divided Family*, 163.

retained the authority in the household. With the understanding that Zeke would never take up arms against the Union, he was given land and received training for civilian work, honoring his father's authority while in his household. It was a truce, if a somewhat uneasy one.

The Breckinridge situation and family was similar to the Clay family. Robert J. Breckinridge was a Kentucky Unionist. His son, William, was a Confederate soldier and his nephew was the prominent Confederate general John C. Breckinridge. William, in similar fashion to Christopher Clay, stepped in to warn his family of a future raid by Kirby Smith. Smith had sent a letter of protection upon request by William, and Robert was spared a Confederate raid. William stated that, "he would be glad that should they [Confederates] be run out of Kentucky that at least his father would benefit."[29] Although this common usage of letters of protection protected many divided families, even more importantly was the family bond it exhibited; perhaps the most amount of comfort or protection a soldier could provide among the grim loss and devastation, in addition to providing proof of familial loyalty. While the common model was moderate Unionist fathers, in exerting their authority in the household their expression of paternal values did not seem as moderate as their political views. Robert was an outspoken devotee of the Union and was "a

---

[29] Taylor, *The Divided Family*, 155.

bitter enemy of Confederate sympathizers and gave little or no quarter even to those within his own family," despite having two sons in the Union, two sons in the Confederacy, a son-in-law in the Confederacy, and a Confederate general nephew.[30] While the sons seemed more rebellious in politics, yet in favor of compromise when it came to familial aspects, the opposite appeared to hold true for many fathers.

The Bell family is an example of a divided family torn by sorrow and tragedy. In the spring of 1861, Henry Bell wrote home to his Unionist family, calling them Tories for opposing the new Confederacy. Henry called their predominantly Union neighbors heathens. Henry's father, John (James), wrote back

> "We ain't in a heathen land, or warent [weren't] until Alabama went out the Union. I rather be called a Tory," John told his son, "than commit such treason against my country." He urged Henry to recall a time when his ancestors marched over frozen ground with bleeding feet to establish the country and secure its liberties. "[I]t is something strange to me that people can

---

[30] (Hutchinson 1965) Jack T. Hutchinson, "Bluegrass and Mountain Laurel: The Story of Kentucky in the Civil War," *Cincinnati Civil War Round Table* (November 1965), http://www.cincinnaticwrt.org/data/ccwrt_history/talks_text/hutchinson_kentucky.html. Web. 2 Dec 2010.

forget the grones and crys of our fourfathers quick."[31]

John's letter illustrates the Constitutional and Republicanism interpretations upon which each side formed their arguments and causes. There are several pieces of correspondence from this family, some of which were Henry's siblings urging him to "change his ways" and return home. Sadly, the family never had an opportunity reconcile their differences. In November 1861, Henry joined the Confederate army while four of his brothers enlisted as Union soldiers. Three brothers did not survive the war. One was killed in battle, another succumbed to "congestive fever," and a third died in prison in Andersonville. Henry died of disease in Chattanooga in 1863.[32]

A less common situation was a family with a Confederate father and a Unionist son. The Morgan family was an example. Judge Thomas Gibbs Morgan of Louisiana was not of the planter class, but did have affluence and owned several black slaves. Although Judge Morgan empathized with Southern rights, he did not support secession, but ultimately

---

[31] Williams, *Bitterly Divided*, 47.

[32] Williams, *Bitterly Divided*, 46-47; Dave Tabler, "I Say Hurrah for Lincoln and the Union Party! The Disunion Party Has Committed Treason," *Appalachian History: Stories, Quotes and Anecdotes* (Feb 9, 2010), http://www.appalachianhistory.net/2010/02/i-say-hurrah-for-lincoln-and-union.html. Web. 4 Dec 2010.

went with the South. This was a very common action among many Southerners. What was unusual, however, was that while the family remained predominantly Southern sympathizers, one of Thomas' sons, Philip Hickey Morgan, became a Union soldier. Although still a divided loyalty situation, the dynamics were sometimes different with a Unionist family and a Rebel son than a Confederate family with a Yankee son. With the Civil War fought predominantly on the South's doorstep, the presence of a Yankee "traitor" in the family seemed to receive more censure. Thomas' others sons, Gibbes, George, and James, served the Confederacy. The youngest son, Harry, died in a duel just as the war began. Thomas died shortly after the war from health-related issues. This left the mother and her daughters, among them Sarah, to maintain the household during the war.

Sarah kept a diary, often discussing how the war had disrupted their family and the issues caused by the divided loyalties. She often received criticism and accusations from Southern neighbors, especially about her Union brother. Sara showed familial support, a common theme among divided families, when defending her brother, in retort to their taunts, "If he is for the Union, it is because he believes it to be in the right, and I honor him for acting from conviction, rather than dread of public opinion."[33] Sarah experienced ambivalence

33 Randall C. Jimerson, *The Private Civil War: Popular Thought During the Sectional Conflict*, (Louisiana State University

toward the North throughout the war. Before the war began, she admitted, "I don't believe in Secession, but I do in Liberty. I want the South to conquer, dictate its own terms, and go back to the Union, for I believe that, apart, inevitable ruin awaits both."[34] Atypical of many Southern sympathizers, Sarah did not believe everyone in the North was evil, but by 1863, her sentiments changed and she viewed Union soldiers as enemies. Later when she and other Confederate women jeered at and spit upon Union soldiers, she felt guilty and realized they were not barbaric as she had allowed her to be convinced from narrow-mindedness and bigotry. The presence of many Union soldiers in her city also affected her sentiments. Sarah was popular and social, and Union men were practically the only men of her age in the area. However, when Union soldiers ransacked her home, her opinion once again changed. This family is typical of the numerous divided loyalties, wavering sentiments, and issues caused by divided loyalties; however, they are also typical in proving that blood really was thicker than water and families healed many of these deep wounds in post-Civil War.

Aside from brother against brother, and father against son, were other similar situations, although usually less contentious than the household males pitted against each other. There are many accounts of wives opposed to husbands, sisters

Press, 1994), 151.

[34] Jimerson, *The Private Civil War*, 151.

turning around or removing pictures of their brothers viewed as fighting on the "wrong" side, a husband who had his wife committed to insane asylum because of her opposing views, and many who sent relatives off to great distances. This latter situation was common as spouses and relatives were sent to distant places or relatives' homes, even overseas, sometimes not just for safety but also because of the embarrassment of opposing sentiments in the household.

It is difficult to determine which families reconciled, since the best primary sources from citizens that vividly display their lives and mindsets, for the most part, ended with the war. It can be hoped that other families like the Campbells, Clays, and even the Prentiss brothers (who almost missed their opportunity to reconcile and offer respect to the other's stance), is the majority sampling. These families' accounts, which showed resiliency and the need to heal the country as well as the family unit, are encouraging.

In the Reconstruction era, as the nation began healing, so did families, as they forgave, compromised, and healed the many wounds. Many families proved to be remarkably resilient, as the nation also proved to be. Some attempted to keep some peace during the war, some began during the war to mend fences, some would be unable to make peace after the war, and still others would never reconcile. Some like the Bell family would never have the opportunity. Accounts are encouraging that a great many of these families picked up the pieces, sought comfort in familial ties, realizing the healing process could begin sooner if these efforts were made.

Cashin summarizes her book with, "[T]he same personal family loyalties that gave way to and even fed the turmoil of war also provided the strongest basis for reconciliation. The divided border state family proved remarkably resilient even as it was most tested, and perhaps for that reason became a cultural resource for a nation also trying to come to terms with the meaning of rebellion."[35] As David Jones illustrates with the Prentiss brother situation, "Each died for his cause in opposition to the other, but in final measure, their spirit of brotherhood prevailed."[36] The family units would endure, albeit forever changed, as was the nation.

"Two girls waiting by the railroad tracks,

For their darlings to come back,

One wore blue, and one wore black."

- *"Two Brothers" by Irving Gordon*

---

[35] Cashin, *The War Was You and Me*, 360.

[36] Jones, *Two Brothers*.

Bibliography

Cashin, Joan E. The War Was You and Me: Civilians in the
        American Civil War. Princeton: Princeton University
        Press, 2002.

Greene, A. Wilson. The Final Battles of the Petersburg
        Campaign: Breaking the Backbone of the Rebellion.
        Mason City: University of Tennessee Press, 2008.

Hutchinson, Jack T. "Bluegrass and Mountain Laurel: The
        Story of Kentucky in the Civil War." Cincinnati Civil
        War Round Table. November 1965.
        http://www.cincinnaticwrt.org/data/ccwrt_history/talks
        _text/hutchinson_kentucky.html (accessed December 2,
        2010).

Jimerson, Randall C. The Private Civil War: Popular Thought
        During the Sectional Conflict. Louisiana State
        University Press, 1994.

Johnston, Editor, Terry A., Alexander Campbell, and James
        Campbell. Him on the one side and me on the other: the
        Civil War letters of Alexander Campbell, 79th New
        York Infantry Regiment and James Campbell, 1st South
        Carolina Battalion. Columbia: Univ of South Carolina
        Press, 1999.

Jones, David H. "Two Brothers: One North, One South."
        David H Jones Reading Groups. 2009.
        http://www.davidhjones.net/frontend_images/userfiles/
        ReadingGroups3.pdf (accessed November 28, 2010).

McKenzie, Robert Tracy. Lincolnites and Rebels: A Divided
        Town in the American Civil War. New York: Oxford
        University Press US, 2006.

McPherson, James M, and James K Hogue. Ordeal by Fire:
        The Civil War and Reconstruction, 4 ed. Boston:
        McGraw-Hill, 2009.

Shaffer, John W. Union and Confederate Soldiers and
        Sympathizers in Barbour County, West Virginia.

Sheehan-Dean, Aaron. Why Confederates Fought: Family and
        Nation in Civil War Virginia. ReadHowYouWant.com,
        2009.

Tabler, Dave. "I say hurrah for Lincoln and the Union party! The Disunion party has committed treason." Appalachian History: Stories, Quotes and Anecdotes. February 9, 2010. http://www.appalachianhistory.net/2010/02/i-say-hurrah-for-lincoln-and-union.html (accessed December 4, 2010).

Taylor, Amy Murrell. The Divided Family in Civil War America. University of North Carolina Press, 2005.

Taylor, John M. "Sibling Rivalry." Civil War Times 38, no. 5 (1999): 65.

Walsh, Kevin. Forgotten New York: Views of a Lost Metropolis. New York: Harper Collins, 2006.

William J. Hamilton, III. "Brother Against Brother at Secessionville." Civil War Preservation Trust. 2009. http://www.civilwar.org/battlefields/secessionville/secessionville-history-articles/brother-against-brother-at.html (accessed November 16, 2010).

Williams, David. Bitterly Divided: The South's Inner Civil War. New York: The New Press, 2010.

The Highland Clearances: The Hills are Empty

Diane Alexander

The Highland Clearances, an event in Scotland's history, has been a largely debated and emotionally charged topic for the last few centuries. The Clearances share vast similarities with the depopulation and removals of indigenous peoples in Australia, Africa and the Americas during the heyday of empire building in the nineteenth century. They have been most closely likened to the Native American Removals and these "evictions" have become "badges of identity" for both groups. Yet, there remain differences in the memorialization of these diasporas in today's historiographies, as well as between the diasporas themselves. What was different in the Highland Clearances from the colonization of numerous other indigenous groups around the globe? Providing a definitive historiography of the Highland Clearances proves a difficult, if not practically impossible, task. This paper explores the cost of these depopulated peoples as consequences of empire-building tactics and victims of marginalized ethnic groups, against the advantages of agricultural and land reform, which greatly benefited the Scottish Highlands and helped bring Britain out of a recession. The Highland Clearances depict an era during the eighteenth and nineteenth century Scotland, summarily described as the process and results of agricultural reform in the Scottish Highlands. Its widespread negative general definition is of a time when sheep were preferred over people, and numerous Scottish Highlanders were brutally evicted from their ancestral lands. The true historiography of the Highland Clearances lies somewhere in between the two extremes of ethnic cleansing and an unfortunate consequence of agricultural reform.

In post-Napoleonic wars, the economy slumped, there were massive increases in debt, and Britain was in a recession. The collapse of the clan system following the Battle of Culloden shifted social and economic aspects in Scotland. Landowners had to adjust to changing economical demands, and their estates needed to become profitable. There was no need for clan chiefs to raise military forces for the Empire after the '45; consequently, the practice of leasing land to kin and the need for clan loyalty diminished. The land had always been held at will, and because the tenants had no guarantees of tenure, they could likewise be evicted at will. Although the Battle of Culloden is often used as the demarcation line of clearances of Scottish Highlanders, there is evidence that the economy had already begun to shift as early as a century before. Thomas Devine in *Clanship to Crofter's War* asserts the Highlands were already in transition and they "were in the throes of a long transition from clanship to commercialism well before the '45."[1]

---

[1] Thomas Martin Devine, *Clanship to Crofter's War: The*

Clans and tacksmen (kin to clan chief that received tacks of land and subsequently subleased to their kin) increasingly were being squeezed out of Scotland's economic structure. Landowners turned toward the competitive market economy and "cleared" many of their tenants in lieu of higher bidders, elbowing out the middleman. As the clan system was replaced with the new market economies, crofters were cleared or moved to other areas, often to the non-arable coastlines where subsistence was substantially difficult. The rise of the kelp industry supplemented many of these evicted coastal dwellers, however, in postwar Britain, the kelp industry plummeted, driving many crofters to starvation. The introduction of hardy sheep, namely the Cheviots, allowed estates to finally run at a profit and meet the economy's demands; however, this action necessitated the clearing of vast numbers of peoples from the lands. Whether many of these landowners took this new market path out of greed or necessity remains a hot topic in Clearance historiography.

The historiographies of the Clearances range from ethnic cleansing by brutal, cruel oppression at gunpoint and fire, to descriptions of the success of agricultural reform and needed improvements in the Scottish Highlands. Some historians, such as John Prebble, describe the Clearances as ruthless, writing the "story of how the Highlanders were deserted and then betrayed.

Social Transformation of the Scottish Highlands, (Manchester, UK: Manchester University Press ND, 1994), 15.

It concerns itself with people, how sheep were preferred to them, and how bayonet, truncheon and fire were used to drive them from their homes."[2] Similar to Prebble's description is Charles Fraser-Macintosh, who states, "[S]ince the introduction of sheep into the Highlands, and before rapacious Lowland sheep farmers, the people disappear as surely as the Red Indians from the advance of the Whites."[3] Paul Basu in *Highland Homecomings: Genealogy and Heritage Tourism in the Scottish Diaspora* details it further, stating:

> In the last 270 years, more than a quarter of million indigenous people were forced off their ancestral lands, burned out of their homes, sold into slavery, and forcibly assimilated into a foreign culture. But these were not Native Americans, or black Africans, or Jews; these were the white residents of the Scottish Highlands. Their crime: Occupying land others coveted.[4]

Colin Calloway saw a parallel between the depopulations of the Scottish Highlanders and Native Americans. Although he decried the treatment of these two groups, he provides a more pragmatic view in *White People, Indians, and Highlanders,*

---

[2] Quoted in Marjory Harper, *Emigrant Homecomings: The Return Movement of Emigrants, 1600-2000.* (Manchester, UK: Manchester University Press, 2005), 136.

[3] Quoted in Paul Basu, *Highland Homecomings: Genealogy and Heritage Tourism in the Scottish Diaspora.* (London: Routledge Taylor & Francis Group, 2007), 201.

[4] Basu, *Highland Homecomings,* 201.

stating, "In Britain, replacing subsistence economy with market-oriented production was regarded as fundamental, both to integrate the Highlands into the larger national economy and to advance the social improvement and "civilization" of the Highlanders."[5] He, additionally, more neutrally infers that the Clearances were responses to the economic changes sweeping Western Europe.

At the other end of the debate are social historians such as Henry Gray Graham, who maintains there was no direct relationship between the volume of outward migration from the Highlands and the success and benefits of scientific progress and greatly needed improvements. Closely related in viewpoint is progressive agriculturist, Sir John Sinclair, founder of the Scottish Agriculture Society, who saw the Highlands as an anachronism in the current economy and in desperate need of reforms. Sinclair is credited with the introduction of the Cheviot breed of sheep to the Highlands, and revolutionary agrarian reforms.[6] Historians such as Graham and Sinclair conspicuously take their place at the other end of the debate, accused by many of extolling the virtues of economy and land reform while deliberately ignoring the social suffering and consequences from such improvements. Parallels are found in the United States

---

⁵ Colin Gordon Calloway, *White People, Indians, and Highlanders: Tribal Peoples and Colonial Encounters in Scotland and America*, (Oxford University Press, 2008), 57.

⁶ McNeil, Kenneth McNeil, *Scotland, Britain, Empire: Writing the Highlands, 1760-1860*, (Columbus: Ohio State University Press, 2007), 5.

when analyzing the diverse viewpoints in the removals of American Indians, in purported need of both civilization and land reform. "Improvers" from both empires tended to believe that any peoples who did not use the land to what they believed was the best use were uncivilized and needed to be removed to make way for those who felt they held the best prescription for progress.

The vast majority of historiographies of Scottish Highland Clearances remain in the median of these opposing ideologies, although few historians would dispute that more often than not violent methods were used to clear the population. The paradox remains of what the Highland Clearances' rightful historiography is. The combinations of lack of written histories and indistinguishable migratory patterns during this Age of Expansion convolute the true story of the Clearances. Comments such as by a Vancouver woman, Christiana, quoted by Paul Basu in *Highland Homecomings: Genealogy and Heritage Tourism in the Scottish Diaspora*, "I don't think Scotland will ever be completely whole until the question of the clearances is put to rest," indicate the true historiography is far from being resolved, and suggests the Clearances will remain eternally in history with divided viewpoints.[7]

It was easy to fall in or out of favor during empire building, above all for the colonized, and favor largely depended on what side of progress and advancement one stood. Scottish

---

[7] Quoted in Basu, *Highland Homecomings*, 190.

Highlanders were no different, having received the broad spectrum of reputations throughout history, ranging from disreputable savages to brave, worthy supporters of the Empire. British colonists "increasingly saw themselves as not just legally but biologically superior to other races" and any perceived attacks upon their selves were dismissed as "*bien peasants* who had no experience or understanding of colonial conditions."[8]

Scots were part of the Celtic peripheries of the British Isles, credited with driving the pagan Picts and Vikings out of the Empire, bringing Christianity to the Isles, and instrumental participants of improvements during the Dark Ages. Despite these accomplishments, Highlanders were largely labeled as backward, savage people, predominantly during the Stuart and Hanoverian Age of Britain, living in primitive places whose "notions of virtue and vice, are very different, from the more Civiliz'd part of Mankind."[9] As early as the fourteenth century, Highlanders began gaining a reputation of savage and untamed peoples, John of Fordun, Aberdeen Chronicler, denouncing them as "beyond the pale of civilization."[10] Many within the Empire adopted this same bias. Ethnocentric colonizers viewed all tribal people as living in savage states and in desperate need of uplifting; and they took these missionary efforts seriously. The

---

[8] Niall Ferguson, *Empire: The Rise and Demise of the British World Order and the Lessons for Global Power*, (New York: Basic Books, 2004), 163.

[9] Calloway, *White People, Indians, and Highlanders*, 61.

[10] Quoted in Devine, *Clanship to Crofter's War*, 2

Scottish Enlightenment propelled this ideology to the forefront, the "improvers" declaring that if tribal people were to survive in this new age, "they would have to be remade in the image of their colonizers."[11] Dr. Johnson, is quoted in *White People, Indians, and Highlanders* speaking to a Scot, "We have taught you, and we'll do the same in time to all barbarous nations."[12] In the same work, Oglethorpe is quoted describing his military forces in the Americas as "White people [,] Indians and highlanders." As Calloway points out, Oglethorpe thought nothing of making a distinction between Scots and whites, stating further, "[it] made sense to eighteenth-century Englishmen."[13] Simply, the British believed they were born to rule and that they knew best.

Not everyone approved of such highly ethnocentric views. General Stewart of Garth's "Sketches of the Highlanders" laments such iniquities during the height of the Clearances, wondering how the British Empire, with her reputation of raising up the oppressed, could so bitterly denounced her own children. Stewart states, "[the Empire] owed their position and their lands to the ancestors of the very men they were no treating so cruelly."[14] According to John Pocock in *The Discovery of Islands: Essays in British History*, "The expansion of Anglo-

---

[11] Calloway, *White People, Indians, and Highlanders*, 60.

[12] Calloway, *White People, Indians, and Highlanders*, 60.

[13] Calloway, *White People, Indians, and Highlanders*, xi.

[14] Janet Mackay, "Highland Clearances," *Electric Scotland*, http://www.electricscotland.com/history/hclearances.htm (accessed April 29, 2011).

Norman – now English – control to nearly all parts of the Atlantic archipelago was completed by the first half of the eighteenth century. Scottish Gaelic society was effectively subdued, though it was not to be physically extinguished until the Highland Clearances of 100 years later."[15]

The majority of improvements and "raising up of culture" occurred during the eighteenth century. By the late nineteenth century, Highlanders, largely due to romanticized and popular histories, came back into favor; however, not before they would pay the price of expansionism. By the nineteenth century, all seemed forgotten or dismissed of Scottish extensive contributions to empire, and Highlanders were relegated to the bottom rung in Anglo-Saxon strata. This social position would greatly impact the effects of the Clearances on these peoples.

Despite the paternalistic bias and treatment of Scots during this era, one fundamental difference remains that set them apart from numerous other colonized global natives – Highlanders were, after all, Christian and Anglo-Saxon. Ethnocentrism still demanded that anyone standing in the way of progress or holding assets valuable to expansionism be treated as thus: if you were not part of the solution, you were the problem. One of the most largely contested disputes in the Clearances debate is to what degree the Highlanders inferior status played, or whether the agricultural reforms were simply an unrelated

---

[15] John Greville Agard Pocock, *The Discovery of Islands: Essays in British History*, Cambridge, UK: Cambridge University Press, 2005), 39.

necessary and crucial event needed to preserve the Empire's economy.

An integral component in the Clearances historiography is the shift from the feudal system practiced in Scotland since ancient times. Clan chiefs would parcel out their estates to tacksmen, usually their kin, and the intermediaries in the feudal landholding structure. These tacksmen would hold the land in exchange for a fixed payment and certain obligations, such as raising military forces when needed. Under this feudal system, law thus confirmed land rights. This system began to falter in the modern economic model. As larger clans extended their territory through wars and populations increased, the distribution of land and its control became proportionately more difficult. Thomas Douglas, Earl of Selkirk, explained the precarious nature of this system, stating, "Those who acquired it by the sword one day were just as likely to lose it in the next." Devine concurs that a kin-based society was volatile, at best, particularly concerning land rights.[16]

Seventeenth and eighteenth century Scotland portrayed the epitome of a societal clash with old meeting new. Land and social status were rapidly changing, threatening old ways and tradition. Reluctance to accept change is demonstrated by Devine

> There seems to have been a general understanding
> that the chief should provide land for his
> clansmen rather than they had rights to specific

---

[16] Devine, *Clanship to Crofter's War*, 9.

individual holdings in perpetuity. …ruling families had the responsibility to act as their protectors and guarantee secure possession of land in return for allegiance, military service, tribute and rental. It was a powerful and enduring belief which lived on long after the military rationale of clanship itself had disappeared and tribal chiefs had shed their ancient responsibilities and become commercial landlords.[17]

This resistance to a change in tradition and ancestral land rights set the stage for Highland Clearances historiography. It is precisely this clash that marks the diverse versions of this era in Scotland's history.

At the height of empire building were progressives such as John Locke who supported colonization with theories such as "terra nullius" demanding that labor be mixed and joined with land; or in other words, if land was not fenced and farmed, it was up for grabs.[18] Indigenous peoples, particularly Native Americans and Scottish Highlanders, were victims of different versions of this concept. A version of *terra nullius* began slowly in the Highlands with improvement and enclosures. Locke's theories were among popular ones in both the British Empire and the United States. In the land rights debate and the concurrent denouncement of tribes and clans, T. Hartley Crawford,

---

[17] Devine, *Clanship to Crofter's War*, 11.
[18] Ferguson, *Empire*, 55.

commissioner of Indian affairs in 1838, is quoted in *White People, Indians, and Highlanders*, "Common property and civilization cannot co-exist."[19] As Calloway points out, this speech was made when the Highland Clearances and Indian Removals were "in full swing, and he could have been speaking for attitudes on both sides of the Atlantic."[20] Economic pressures and postwar effects would escalate to forced emigration and evictions. A combination of the sharp decline in the kelp industry postwar, escalating improvements but little land for the entire population, and the potato famine in 1846, caused a push toward emigration; and many that did not were forced. The Clearances reached their apex at this time.

Various landowners in the Highlands implemented new enlightened suggestions of enclosure and improvements, some with great success. Enclosures and improvements saw betterment in land rights, survival, and stability of tenants to farm the land. The leases for land were longer-term contracts, and there were specific agricultural directions on how best to enclose and improve the lands. Some cases, such as in Monymusk, demonstrated the redistribution of lands with the least harmful effects on the peoples. However, this was not the norm in any means. Notwithstanding the success of such models, as with the clan system, there simply was not enough land to meet the population's need.

---

[19] Quoted in Calloway, *White People, Indians, and Highlanders*, 57.

[20] Calloway, *White People, Indians, and Highlanders*, 57.

Some estates were notorious for their brutal evictions, notably the Sutherland and Skye estates. Donald MacLeod, a Sutherland crofter and stonemason, whose works occupy a predominant place in the Scottish Clearances history, was eyewitness to chaos, burning, and cries of women and children. As quoted in Anthony Adolph's *Tracing Your Scottish History*, Sutherland reports "a large portion of the people of these parishes were in the course of two or three years, almost entirely rooted out, and those few who took miserable allotments…and some of their descendants continue to exist on them in great poverty."[21] In Skye, the clearances were also particularly brutal, evicting over 40,000 people, many old and feeble, including an "81 year old and 3 week old baby forced out in the cold."[22] In Skye alone, there were 1700 writs issued, and evictions of 2,000 families in one day were not uncommon.[23] Basu, quoting Christina again in *Highland Homecomings*, writes, "We really didn't see that much difference between what happened in the Highlands to the Gaels and what happened in North America to the Native Indian population, quoted Christina again. Except that the Indians were not actually expelled from their continent."[24]

Notwithstanding the documented brutal evictions, another hot topic and crucial component of the effects of the

---

[21] Adolph, Anthony Adolph, *Tracing Your Scottish Family History*, Buffalo: Firefly Books, 2009), 149.

[22] *A History of Scotland - This Land Is Our Land.* Directed by Clara Glynn. Hosted by Neil Oliver. 2009.

[23] *A History of Scotland*, Neil Oliver.

[24] Basu, *Highland Homecomings*, 190.

Clearances was emigration. Many historians complain of obfuscating historiographies by incorrectly interpreting migration numbers and patterns. Many historians caution that depictions of the Clearances that drove Scottish masses from their homes needs to be evaluated from all angles. Some argue that the brutality and oppression of evicting her people caused Scotland's hallmark of shame and depopulation. Statements such as "Highlanders after the post-45 clearances, fled [to] America in droves," indicates "abstract deduction from mistaken premises" according to Berthoff. Many historians argue that Highland Scots were well on the move long before the Clearances. According to Graham,

> The immigrants who fled before the Highland clearances of 1790-1890, the century of evictions for sheep pasture, were poor crofters whose resistance to assimilation in their new country was much less than that of their eighteenth-century [Revolutionary] forebears. After the Revolution, Highland immigration to the United States grew in volume with each succeeding decade. Checked first by the first French war (1793-1801) and by the War of 1812, the Highlanders recommenced the flow as soon as peace came."[25]

---

[25] Ian Charles Cargill Graham, *Colonists from Scotland: Emigration to North America, 1707-1783,* (Baltimore: Genealogical Publishing Com, 2009), 181.

As early as the 1630s, the number of Scots in Ulster more than doubled by immigration from the interior Highlands between Aberdeenshire and Inverness. In later seventeenth century, vast numbers of new Scottish incomers to Ulster were "presumably from the areas that had supplied the earlier immigrants and so were also largely Highlanders."[26]

Still others claim the Clearances accelerated the process, but emigration was already in place because of the deterioration of the clan system, begun even before the Battle of Culloden. Yet others claim there remains no relation between the agricultural reforms and emigrant Scots. It seems impossible to discern how much responsibility to assign to the infamous replacement of peoples with sheep with the emigration of Scottish Highlanders. The migration numbers seem to prove that emigration was well in place long before the Clearances, with the evictions accelerating those who were now being forced out.

Reform acts and finally the 1886 Crofter's Act marked the official end of the Clearances. The Crofters Act, 25 June 1886, "allowed crofter and cottar alike the "Three Fs (fair rents, fixity of tenure and free sale), so that holding could be passed down in the family, with a Crofters' Commission to adjudicate on fair rents.[27] The linchpin of the Highland Clearances debate is summed up succinctly by Ian Graham in *Colonists from Scotland: Emigration to North America, 1707-1783*, "The

---

[26] Berthoff, Rowland Berthoff, "Celtic Mist over the South," *The Journal of Southern History* 52, no. 4 (1986): 536.

[27] Adolph, *Tracing Your Scottish Family History*, 153.

problem of the eighteenth-century Highland evictions is, paradoxically, inseparable from that of the agrarian improvements of the period.[28] Some argue pragmatically that even had the landowners made herculean efforts to make improvements while mitigating the plight of the masses, it would have had little effect. As Graham further states, "[T]here remained the fundamental problem of the pressure of population upon the means of subsistence. The surplus population of wholly or partially unemployed persons would still have remained as the single greatest cause of poverty."[29] Overpopulation and stifling poverty were legitimate dire concerns, supporting the historians of viewpoints that agricultural reforms were fundamentally crucial to Scotland and likely her plight would have been considerably worse had these improvements not been implemented.

One fundamental difference between the Scottish Highlanders and other colonized peoples during the Age of Expansion is the end result. The outcome for cleared Highlanders turned out noticeably more favorable than did the removed Native Americans. Both groups lost their ancestral grounds, often in brutal methods, and yet the Highlanders, many expelled to another continent, seemed to emerge from the colonial projects and expansionism remarkably more unscathed than other colonized peoples. For the cleared Highlanders, along

---

[28] Graham, *Colonists from Scotland*, 51.

[29] Graham, *Colonists from Scotland*, 54.

with the blighted potato farmers in Ireland, the emigrations will always represent a cruel and oppressive time in their history. The Scottish Highlands experienced a depopulation of up to three-quarters of the population, while other continents, particularly North America, reveal where the peoples repopulated. For many of these Scottish immigrants, the United States offered better lives than the overcrowded, poverty-stricken non-arable lands offered to Scots during two centuries. Whether evicted or in search of a better life, substantial numbers of Scottish immigrants exerted great influence on new lands in America; their role in the history of American provinces "clearly distinguishable" from that of other immigrant groups.[30] The oppressed Scottish Highlanders had more fortune on their side – in the ethnocentric empire building game, they were the right color and immigration to the United States came at a fortunate time for a new life in a land offering life, liberty and freedom. Freedom would not apply to all her citizens until the twentieth century; such delayed rights incurring an extremely high cost for Native Americans, and thus justifying the contrasting outcomes of these two groups. In an ironic twist, the Native Americans had land rights on their side, in addition to not being expelled to a different continent, and yet they emerged much more marginalized and scarred than did the Scottish Highlanders.

The American South and the Appalachia region is highly representative of peoples of Scottish ancestry. Vestiges of

---

[30] Graham, *Colonists from Scotland*, 183.

centuries of immigrant Highlanders is seen in culture, folklore, agricultural, music, storytelling, kinship concepts, political views, and even the geography itself, many places in the Appalachians similar to the Scottish Highlands. Whether due to forced emigration or voluntary migration during the era of the Clearances, significant numbers of Highlanders emigrated to North America and Australia, where today more descendants of Highlanders are found than in Scotland itself.[31] Notwithstanding the brutality of this colonial project with its clearings, the Scottish Highlanders exhibited the ability to throw off the colonial yoke and as is their typical hardy constitution, create a home away from home – particularly the Highlands in the American South. It is no coincidence that Appalachia, overrepresented by Scot-Irish in earlier centuries, developed much of the same reputation as the Highlands in previous centuries in Britain – a primitive place, isolated, backward peoples, and as most commonly described: "otherness." The fact that the United States, as a child of the British Empire, in its American Indian removals in full swing at the same time as the British Empire was removing many of her indigenous peoples is no coincidence. The United States adopted many political and cultural from her parent, and during the Age of Expansion, she adopted many of her peoples as well.

---

[31] "Highland Clearances," *Crann Tara*, March 5, 2009, http://www.cranntara.org.uk/clear.htm (accessed April 11, 2011).

Countless Americans today feel fortunate their ancestors "crossed the pond" to form new homes, supporting Tamara Kohn's assertion in "Becoming an Islander through Action in the Scottish Hebrides" when people move away, they don't lose their identity…identity and kinship are acquired through activity in the present.[32] Roy Alexander, in *Power Speech*, is like-minded, stating "When it came to oral history, believe me, these people had plenty to talk about. From the hill pockets of Wales, the wild moors of Ireland, and the highlands of Scotland, my ancestors settled in Appalachian valleys under the shadow of peaks higher than any in eastern America…Proud and cantankerous, this Appalachian race hewed to a life as relentlessly as pine roots growing through granite."[33] The Highland Clearances remain a romanticized and identity for those of Scottish ancestry, and are told in beautiful, gripping detail as Scots do best with their renowned storytelling prowess. Their music rituals still today are highly representative of their tradition of oral history. Tom Brown, in "Sugar in the Gourd: Preserving Appalachian Tradition," observes the music culture of these transplanted Highlanders, stating, "[a] prominent part of Southern Mountain life…authentic folk musicians who are living links in oral tradition."[34]

---

[32] Tamara Kohn, "Becoming an Islander through Action in the Scottish Hebrides," *The Journal of the Royal Anthropological Institute* 8, no. 1 (March 2002): 154

[33] Alexander, Roy Alexander, *Power Speech: The Quickest Route to Business and Personal Success*, (New York: Amacom American Management Association, 1986), 5.

Prebble states, "It has been said that the Clearances are now far enough away from us to be decently forgotten. But the hills are still empty...."[35] The Appalachian hills are not. Peoples of Scottish Highlander ancestry can be found in many corners of the world, predominantly the United States, Canada, and Australia. The cost of expansionism for numerous emigrant Scots was outweighed by benefits in a new land. For the Scots who remained in their homelands, whether the price of progress came at too great a cost for Scotland largely remains a contested discussion.

---

[34] Tom Brown, "Sugar in the Gourd: Preserving Applachian Traditions." *Music Educators Journal* 70, no. 3 (November 1983): 53.

[35] Basu, *Highland Homecomings*, 189.

Bibliography

Adolph, Anthony. Tracing Your Scottish Family History.
        Buffalo: Firefly Books, 2009.

Alexander, Roy. Power Speech: The Quickest Route to Business
        and Personal Success. New York: Amacom American
        Management Association, 1986.

Basu, Paul. Highland Homecomings: Genealogy and Heritage
        Tourism in the Scottish Diaspora. London: Routledge
        Taylor & Francis Group, 2007.

Berthoff, Rowland. "Celtic Mist over the South." The Journal of
        Southern History 52, no. 4 (1986): 523-546.

Brown, Tom. "Sugar in the Gourd: Preserving Applachian
        Traditions." Music Educators Journal (MENC: The
        National Association for Music Education) 70, no. 3
        (November 1983): 52-55.

Calloway, Colin Gordon. White People, Indians, and
        Highlanders: Tribal Peoples and Colonial Encounters in
        Scotland and America. Oxford University Press, 2008.

Devine, Thomas Martin. Clanship to Crofter's War: The Social
        Transformation of the Scottish Highlands. Manchester,
        UK: Manchester University Press ND, 1994.

Ferguson, Niall. Empire: The Rise and Demise of the British
        World Order and the Lessons for Global Power. New
        York: Basic Books, 2004.

Gerald Newman, Leslie Ellen Brown. Britain in the Hanoverian
        age, 1714-1837: An Encylopedia (Volume 1481 of
        Garland reference library of the humanities). Taylor &
        Francis, 1997.

A History of Scotland - This Land Is Our Land. Directed by
        Clara Glynn. Hosted by Neil Oliver. 2009.

Graham, Ian Charles Cargill. Colonists from Scotland:
        Emigration to North America, 1707-1783. Baltimore:
        Genealogical Publishing Com, 2009.

Harper, Marjory. Emigrant Homecomings: The Return
        Movement of Emigrants, 1600-2000. Manchester, UK:
        Manchester University Press, 2005.

"Highland Clearances." Crann Tara. March 5, 2009.
        http://www.cranntara.org.uk/clear.htm (accessed April
        11, 2011).

Kohn, Tamara. "Becoming an Islander through Action in the
     Scottish Hebrides." The Journal of the Royal
     Anthropological Institute 8, no. 1 (March 2002): 143-
     158.

Mackay, Janet, contributor. "Highland Clearances." Electric
     Scotland. April 21, 2011.
     http://www.electricscotland.com/history/hclearances.htm
     (accessed April 29, 2011).

McNeil, Kenneth. Scotland, Britain, Empire: Writing the
     Highlands, 1760-1860. Columbus: Ohio State University
     Press, 2007.

Pocock, John Greville Agard. The Discovery of Islands: Essays
     in British History. Cambridge, UK: Cambridge
     University Press, 2005.